Live Forever

The John and Robin Dickson Series in Texas Music
Sponsored by the Center for Texas History,
Texas State University
Jason Mellard, General Editor

Billy Joe Shaver, by Mandy Newham-Cobb.

Live Forever

The Songwriting Legacy of Billy Joe Shaver

Courtney S. Lennon

TEXAS A&M UNIVERSITY PRESS
COLLEGE STATION

This paper meets the requirements of ANSI/NISO Z39.48-1992
(Permanence of Paper).
Binding materials have been chosen for durability.
Manufactured in the United States of America

Library of Congress Cataloging-in-Publication Data

Names: Lennon, Courtney S., author. | Atkinson, Brian T., writer of
    foreword. | Bare, Bobby, writer of foreword.
Title: Live forever: the songwriting legacy of Billy Joe Shaver / Courtney
    S. Lennon.
Other titles: John and Robin Dickson series in Texas music.
Description: First edition. | College Station: Texas A&M University Press,
    [2022] | Series: John and Robin Dickson series in Texas music | Includes
    index.
Identifiers: LCCN 2021040353 (print) | LCCN 2021040354 (ebook) | ISBN
    9781623499549 (cloth) | ISBN 9781623499556 (ebook)
Subjects: LCSH: Shaver, Billy Joe. | Country musicians—Texas—Biography. |
    Lyricists—Texas—Biography. | BISAC: MUSIC / Genres & Styles / Country
    & Bluegrass | MUSIC / Individual Composer & Musician | LCGFT:
    Biographies.
Classification: LCC ML420.S534 L46 2022 (print) | LCC ML420.S534 (ebook)
    | DDC 782.421642092 [B]—dc23
LC record available at https://lccn.loc.gov/2021040353
LC ebook record available at https://lccn.loc.gov/2021040354

Cover photo: Billy Joe Shaver at the Red Ants Pants Music Festival,
White Sulphur Springs, Montana, 2012. Photo by Tony Demin.

*For my fellow writer Donald R. Lennon
and in fond memory of Papa, William C. Gocella*

Contents

Foreword

Bobby Bare

illy Joe Shaver was everything people thought Waylon Jennings was. You never had to wonder what was bothering him. He'd tell you. Billy was your typical Texan—straightforward, straight to the point. A lot of songwriters will do whatever it takes to get a song cut. Billy isn't someone you push around. You're not going to scare him. He's not going to let you. He's a great songwriter and believes in the songs that he writes.

Billy Joe came to my office at the RCA building in Nashville, Tennessee, not long after I started my publishing company. He had written down some songs. I thought, *That's pretty crazy.* I didn't know what to do about it, but I realized his writing was coming from a different direction. It dawned on me how talented he was. He writes the most honest lines. You spend three minutes with him, and you know he's his own unique person.

Billy Joe was the first songwriter I signed. A lot came by. He did that "aw, shucks" thing, but it didn't fool me. Billy Joe was the brightest person in the room. I was maybe paying him fifty dollars a week, enough for him to buy gas for his old pickup truck. He had a key to the office, and he'd sleep there a lot of times. He was probably drunk. I recorded "Ride Me Down Easy," Waylon Jennings did *Honky Tonk Heroes*, and then John Anderson did "I'm Just an Old Chunk of Coal (but I'm Gonna Be a Diamond Someday)." Those three triggered his career. Billy Joe was the real deal, the Texas outlaw.

Bobby Bare, interview with Courtney S. Lennon, July 26, 2018.
See also www.bobbybare.com.

Foreword

Brian T. Atkinson

Billy Joe Shaver's earthy yarns link sacred and secular with a devil's grin. "Faith gets in there every doggone time I write a song," he once told me. "I don't wanna say anything bad about it, man, but it gets me looking like some preacher. Waylon Jennings called me a Bible thumper. I said, 'I'll thump you, buddy.'" Man, read those words over again and tell me there's another who better embodies Kris Kristofferson's protagonist from "The Pilgrim: Chapter 33," who's "a walking contradiction, partly truth and partly fiction." Shaver's here, there, and everywhere. He prays. He sins. He searches for the demons within. Then he writes songs—peaceful and pure, complex and convoluted, mad and merciful—that everyone perfectly understands. See why Bob Dylan name-checked him in a song?

Dylan gets it. He always does. Shaver's songs might not look like much on the surface. Their language remains common. The arrangements simple. Melodies easy. Then they sneak through the side door and stick you up. You'll take notice then, buddy. This simple man—the wacko from Waco, whatever you want to call him—might be the smartest of them all. The most poetic. We wouldn't have him in this songwriter series if he wasn't. Billy Joe Shaver belongs right alongside Townes Van Zandt, Ray Wylie Hubbard, Mickey Newbury, and all the rest who will eventually find a home here. Please welcome my friend Courtney S. Lennon into your homes. Her first book for us has earned a special place on your coffee table. Relax and enjoy.

Left to right: Jeremy Lynn Woodall and Billy Joe Shaver performing at Sportsmen's Tavern in Buffalo, New York, July 8, 2014. Photo by Tyler Cooney.

Preface

ust a few months before this book was even a thought, I finished my first novel, *Where Dreams Never Die*. The book is loosely based on my time living in Los Angeles and writing about Texas music. In the opening of the book, I'm sitting there with a character, Thirsty, listening to the album that changed his life. The record I picked was *Honky Tonk Heroes* because that album was my gateway into "real deal" country music. As the record plays, I tell the story of the making of the album verbatim. The last line I wrote about the album was, "And that was the birth of outlaw country." I look back at it now and think, *Did you really open your novel with the Honky Tonk Heroes story, and now you're writing a book on the singular honky-tonk hero himself?* Life is weird.

Of course, it just goes to show how much impact Billy Joe Shaver's music had on my life. I grew up in the country, hating country music because it was the nineties and I had no exposure to Texas country in the middle of nowhere outside Buffalo, New York. The music that I was exposed to, that I liked, came via my parents' record collection in the basement. When I was fourteen, I discovered *Pet Sounds* by the Beach Boys. I was absolutely blown away by this songwriter Brian Wilson. I was fourteen and knew to appreciate the person who wrote the songs and how important that was. Growing up where I did, I was isolated and didn't have anyone to relate to. I wound up making friends online in chatrooms about music, and it seems that to this day most any friend I've made has come from a shared love of music.

I met my dear friend Gary Austin in Los Angeles in 2010 when I was twenty-five and he was sixty-nine. Gary founded the improvisation troupe the Groundlings back in the 1970s. We met in an unconventional way—he was in the hospital undergoing a stem cell transplant. It's a long story how I wound up there. I'd moved out to L.A. to do improvisation, to get me out of my comfort zone. When I met Austin, I figured that we'd talk about that, until one day we came to realize we shared the same favorite songwriter, Townes Van Zandt. It bonded us immediately. Austin was from Texas, and when he got out of the hospital he gave me a good education on Texas music by playing a DVD of the 2007 film *Never Say Die*, Waylon Jennings's final concert. It was bittersweet to see Waylon in poor health, but I was blown away by him and the songs.

I asked Austin what I should listen to by Waylon. He said, *"Honky Tonk Heroes."* I heard that album, and it completely changed the trajectory of what I thought country music could and should be. I saw the name "Billy Joe Shaver" and thought, *Who is this guy that wrote all these songs?* From there, I found a copy of the *Honky Tonk Heroes* album Shaver put out with Willie Nelson and Kris Kristofferson. I heard Shaver do "Texas Uphere Tennessee" and was floored by the energy and his voice that sounds like no one else. Not long after that, I diverged from my musical roots and fully explored country. Shaver bridged the gap. He was special. He could write poetry like Townes did but in a way that somebody like me, who grew up next to a cornfield and cows, can completely relate to. I wound up going to college to study philosophy, and I see the intelligence and the humanistic themes throughout his songs. He knew he wasn't perfect, and he wasn't ashamed to admit that. Not every story in this book puts him on a pedestal, but his faults make me like him more. He was authentic, didn't put up with attitude, and was arguably the greatest country songwriter to have lived. That's why, back in 2012, when Terry Paul Roland came to me at my magazine, *Turnstyled, Junkpiled* (named after the Townes song), with a cover story on Shaver, I said, "Let's do an entire weeklong tribute to Billy Joe." I got together a bunch of musicians to film videos performing their favorite Shaver songs, and years later some of them wound up in this book. I'm not a singer, but that week my grandma Mary had just passed away, so I filmed a short clip of me doing "Live Forever." The emotion that song brings to me is unwavering. Now when I hear that song and know *Live Forever* is now the title of my book about Shaver, I get choked up. What an honor to help, if even in a small way, to preserve his legacy.

This book came about when I was going through some hard times. Austin had passed away just a year before, and I was in a hospital room in North Carolina after my father-in-law, Don Lennon, had a massive stroke. I had known Brian T. Atkinson for years because of our shared love for Townes. When I started *Turnstyled, Junkpiled,* his book, *I'll Be Here in the Morning: The Songwriting Legacy of Townes Van Zandt* had just come out. We did a week for Townes when that book came out, and I always had a great respect for him, for preserving Townes's songs. I was completely surprised when he asked me if I wanted to write one. I thought, *Why would someone do something like that for me?* He told me to pick a subject, and I thought about it. Who was as good as Townes? Billy Joe Shaver.

My father-in-law was a history professor, and he wrote some books, including *A Quest for Glory: Major General Robert Howe and the American Revolution.* In those days in the hospital, he couldn't communicate, but a few months before that, I'd made sure to get him a printed draft of my novel, for him to be the very first to read it. That was our bond: we were both writers. When the Shaver idea came up, I wasn't sure if he could hear me, but I sat beside his hospital bed, holding his hand, and said, "Dad, I want to write a book on Billy Joe Shaver. He's a Christian like you. I'd like your blessing. It's a history book, just like how you wrote, and I'm gonna dedicate it to you. I promise." He passed away a few days later.

Acknowledgments

Thanks to the John and Robin Dickson Series editors, Thom Lemmons at Texas A&M University Press, Jason Mellard, and the Center for Texas Music History for making this book a reality. Thanks to Brian T. Atkinson for paving the way with the Songwriting Legacy series and for all the guidance and encouragement. I couldn't have asked for a better friend and mentor. His book *The Messenger: The Songwriting Legacy of Ray Wylie Hubbard* served as an initial blueprint for this book, which is based almost entirely on primary source interviews. I edited these interviews (conducted from 2018–19) for accuracy, clarity, length, and flow. Thanks to all the artists who took the time to help me celebrate the life and music of Billy Joe Shaver. I hope this book does well in honoring his life and songwriting legacy.

My husband, Mark Whitfield Lennon is always by my side in life and snaps photos on occasion. He helped build *Turnstyled, Junkpiled* from the ground up and acts as managing editor. I appreciate all the support in life and writing. Thanks to all the great writers at *Turnstyled, Junkpiled* for holding down the fort: Kim Grant (who did so much in the early days of the Los Angeles Americana scene with the founding of the Grand Old Echo), Brian Rock, Terry Paul Roland, whose features have blown me away over the past eight years, and artist contributor Mandy Newham-Cobb for again providing a great illustration to go along with my writing.

Thanks to Dwane Hall of the 2018 Ameripolitan Venue of the Year, the Sportsmen's Tavern for hosting so many great acts here in Buffalo, New York, and for all the work he does to keep this music alive. I was lucky enough to see Billy Joe perform there in 2014. Thanks to my fellow honky-tonk heroes in the Buffalo area: Robert McLennan and Elmer Ploetz of the Sportsmen's Americana Foundation and *JAM Magazine*;

Tyler Cooney, who provided me with photos; my friends and singer-songwriters Cody Barcroft and Tyler Westcott for helping keep roots music alive here; and Dan Gailey, who brought Dallas Moore to town twice for private shows. Thanks to Dallas for always making it a point to plow through an entire set of Shaver tunes when in town.

I owe my parents, Robert and Bonnie Sudbrink, for always giving me the freedom to pursue what I'm passionate about, no matter how unconventional, in art, philosophy, improvisation, and writing. Thanks to my second set of folks, Don and Billie Lennon for all the kindness and support. My grandma Jean was named after the Stephen Foster song "I Dream of Jeannie with the Light Brown Hair" because Stephen Foster was her kin. I grew up on his music and was thus exposed to roots music and American songwriting from an early age. My grandpa William "Chet" Gocella, Papa, was my best friend growing up, and a train engineer who let me drive the train on the South Buffalo Railway when I was three. I owe him for my love of trains and train songs. I have his cowboy boots and hat in my office. I remember a time when I was very young and he was wearing one of his black western shirts, and my dad was in black too. I said, "Why are you guys all in black?" He stood there, real serious, and said, "We're going to see Johnny Cash." Like a five-year-old knew what that meant. I'll never forget it.

Live Forever

Introduction

illy Joe Shaver established himself as country music's unsung hero. Shaver was a master songwriter whose temptation-and-tragedy tales have been given breath by such singers as Bob Dylan ("Old Five and Dimers Like Me"), Joe Ely ("Live Forever"), "Cowboy" Jack Clement ("You Asked Me To"), and Bobby Bare ("Ride Me Down Easy"). In 1981, John Anderson went to number four with Shaver's "I'm Just an Old Chunk of Coal (but I'm Gonna Be a Diamond Someday)," a song about his own salvation that serves as proverb and paradigm. "Billy Joe's strength is conveying the complexity of ideas and emotions with eloquent simplicity," explains singer-songwriter Brian Wright, a native of Waco, Texas. "It's a simple way of saying, 'I'm trying to be a better man.'"[1]

Shaver earned high marks from fellow songwriting legends for his effortless authenticity and dedication to his craft over the years. He was "as real a writer as Hemingway. He's timeless," said Kris Kristofferson, who was first to record a Shaver song ("Good Christian Soldier") and produced his 1973 debut, *Old Five and Dimers Like Me*.[2] Shaver, born August 16, 1939, was raised in Corsicana, Texas, by his grandmother Birdie Lee Watson until her death when he was twelve years old.[3] Shaver documented his impoverished childhood in his 1973 recording "I Been to Georgia on a Fast Train." "They say my mammy left me, day before she had me," he sings, explaining why he wound up in Birdie's care, living off social security checks.[4] Two months before Billy Joe was born, his father, a bootlegger named Virgil "Buddy" Shaver, brutally beat Billy Joe's then-teenage mother, Victory "Tincie" Shaver. Virgil stomped on her stomach and left her for dead by a stock tank. There Tincie lay for hours until an old man discovered her bruised and bloodied body.[5] She swore that if her unborn child was a boy, she'd leave him, and she did just that, heading to Waco, Texas, to work as a waitress, eventually landing at Green Gables, the bar immortalized in Shaver's iconic outlaw country anthem "Honky Tonk Heroes," a song first recorded by Waylon Jennings as the title track to his 1973 album.

While Shaver was only in school through eighth grade, his English teacher noticed his gift with words and encouraged him to pursue poetry. Shaver's language, rooted in archaic slang and framed by his rural Texas upbringing, would later help propel his career as he became highly regarded by his peers. "When I got to Nashville, I had people walking behind me with tape recorders," Shaver said in a 2014 interview with *Texas Music* magazine. "I don't intend to be that poetic, but that's just the way I feel."[6] "Billy Joe is Shakespeare in Texas," says singer-songwriter friend Kimmie Rhodes. "He's a phenomenon."[7]

Shaver partly credited his English teacher's encouragement for his career as a songwriter, but he also cited his country music hero Hank Williams, who he saw by chance one evening at the Miracle Bread Company in Corsicana when he was ten years old. Shaver recalled in his 1993 song "Tramp on Your Street" that he walked "ten miles of train track to hear Hank Williams sing."[8] When Shaver snuck out of the house that evening, he wasn't expecting to see Williams (then billed as Luke the Drifter). "I didn't know he was there," Shaver said in a 2012 interview. "They didn't call him 'Luke The Drifter' (that night)," he continued. "They said Hank Williams—and he noticed there wasn't nobody listening to him, and he just looked me right straight in the eye and sang straight to me and just . . . lit me up."[9]

In 1953, Shaver met country music icon Willie Nelson, who at the time was trying to earn a living as a songwriter. "This DJ introduced [us]," Shaver said in a 2012 interview with *Turnstyled, Junkpiled* magazine. "He was playing clubs . . . all up and down the [Dallas] Highway there in Waco. He was all over the place. I loved to listen to him 'cause his lyrics were so great. I was inspired by him. I won't say I was influenced, but he lit a fire under me."[10] While Shaver's song "Willie the Wandering Gypsy and Me" pays homage to Nelson, he didn't initially use the name "Willy" for fear of irritating his best friend. But it was this song that caught the ear of Waylon Jennings, who quietly listened in as Shaver played the tune in a backstage trailer at Nelson's Dripping Springs Reunion Picnic in 1972, which would later be known as Willie's Fourth of July Picnic.[11] "He asked me if I had any more of them cowboy songs," Shaver recalled to Terry Roland in 2012. "I told him I had a sack full of them. He said, 'Well come on up to Nashville and I'll do a whole album of them.'" "I took him at his word and chased him around for six months."[12]

Shaver finally tracked down Jennings at RCA studios in Nashville. When Jennings heard Shaver was there, he sent out Nashville radio disc jockey Roger "Captain Midnight" Schutt, who had arranged for Shaver to be there in the first place, to give Shaver a $100 bill and tell him to hit the road. Shaver returned the cash and told Schutt to tell Waylon to stick it up his ass. Waylon left the control room to confront Shaver and said, "What do you want, Hoss?" Shaver looked directly at him. "You told me to bring some songs. If you don't at least listen to 'em, I'm gonna whip your ass in front of God and everybody."[13] The meeting would change Shaver's life and country music.

The first song he played for Jennings was "Ain't No God in Mexico," a tale from his border-jumping days going to the Matamoros, Mexico, "boys' town" (red-light district) and "gettin' busted by the man," indulging in underage drinking, drugs, and prostitution. The latter topic is also the source of Shaver's song "Black Rose," which historian Bill C. Malone references in the book that is the basis of Ken Burns's PBS documentary *Country Music*: "Shaver came up with one of the best lines used by his rowdy confederates when he noted in a song that 'the devil made me do it the first time, the second time I done it on my own.'"[14]

Jennings was impressed. His 1973 *Honky Tonk Heroes* album would contain ten songs, nine by Shaver, and reach number fourteen on *Billboard*'s Top Country Albums chart. The Shaver-and-Jennings-penned "You Asked Me To" rose to number eight on the Billboard country singles chart. However, Shaver never found such commercial success with his own songs. When he released his debut album, *Old Five and Dimers Like Me*, that same year, "I Been to Georgia on a Fast Train" only made it to number eighty-eight on the charts. While the album may not have been a commercial success, it serves as memoir, and songs like "Jesus Christ What a Man" and "When Jesus Was Our Savior and Cotton Was Our King" set the tone for a career of contradiction, intermingling Shaver's Christian faith with hard living and hardship. "There's nothing more country than Billy Joe Shaver," says singer-songwriter Chuck Mead. "He's in the canon, right up there on the Mount Rushmore of outlaws, with Waylon, Willie, and Tompall Glaser. You can set your watch by *Honky Tonk Heroes*. It was a cornerstone of 1970s music and culture in America."[15]

A 2018 *Washington Post* article pointed out Shaver's lack of success despite his influence with the headline "Billy Joe Shaver Invented Outlaw Country. Why Is He Still Rambling around Texas in a Van?"[16] While the outlaw movement cannot be credited to just one person, Shaver was instrumental.

Still, he never got the recognition his peers did. This is partly due to bad publishing deals and his lack of business sense, but the true existential answer to the question may be found in the lyrics to "Willy the Wandering Gypsy and Me": "Moving's the closest thing to being free."[17]

"Waylon Jennings and Willie Nelson may have been the faces of the outlaw country movement," says South Carolina–based singer-songwriter James Scott Bullard, "but [I believe] Billy Joe Shaver gave birth to it. I don't think anyone could deny that. It's that simple. I don't understand why Billy Joe never got to be a big star like those boys. Kris Kristofferson himself produced *Old Five and Dimers Like Me* because he knew Billy Joe had a gift."[18]

Through the years, Shaver tried to make money off his songs by re-recording his standards on various albums, and he changed the title of "Black Rose" to "The Devil Made Me Do It the First Time" on his 1987 *Salt of the Earth* album to bank on the song's memorable line. In 1993, Shaver teamed up with son Eddy as the band Shaver on the album *Tramp on Your Street*. One of its singles was a rock and roll–infused remake of "I Been to Georgia on a Fast Train," with an accompanying video shown on MTV and CMT. At the time the song came out, Jennings's *Honky Tonk Heroes* was hard to find, and *Tramp on Your Street* brought Shaver's music to a new generation of fans. *Tramp on Your Street* also includes the first studio recording of Shaver's spiritual "Live Forever," a song he revisited in 2005 as a collaboration with fellow Texans and popular country chart-toppers Big & Rich.

"My son Eddy gave me [the melody] way back around 1989," Shaver said in a 2012 interview. "Oh God, it's such a great melody. The melody's so good that I carried it around for six months before I could figure out what to put with it. . . . Nobody recognized it as a great song when it came out. I have a lot of songs that people discover later on. I imagine that I'll be dead and gone a long time before people figure some of these out. If I'd heard one of these songs that I wrote now, I guess I'd just shoot myself if I didn't write it. Man, I just love my songs. They're like kids, though: it's hard to tell which one's the best."[19]

"'Live Forever' is a masterpiece," says Grammy-nominated songwriter David Lee. "All the work that Eddy did on that album with his guitar was awesome. It was loud live. They would come out to the show and blow your hair back."[20] On New Year's Eve 2000, Shaver lost his son Eddy to a heroin overdose. Within the span of a year, he also lost his mother and his wife Brenda whom he had married three times over forty years. "I'm amazed at how he lost his wife and son and keeps going," said longtime friend Rosie Flores.

On August 5, 2014, Shaver released his final studio album, the critically acclaimed *Long in the Tooth* on Lightning Rod Records. After a forty-one-year career, it became his first album to make it into the *Billboard* Top Country Albums chart and includes the Willie Nelson collaboration "Hard to Be an Outlaw," a song inspired by singer-songwriter friend Jackson Taylor. "This is the best album I've ever done," Shaver said. "It's just dangerously good. I expect it to change things and turn things around the way *Honky Tonk Heroes* did."[21]

Billy Joe Shaver suffered a massive stroke on October 27, 2020. While Covid-19 protocol made visits difficult, long-time friend Connie Nelson said in *Texas Monthly* that she spoke to doctors at Waco's Ascension Providence Hospital where Shaver was being cared for and said, "Let [Billy Joe] know Willie and Connie love him so much." They assured her they would. Shaver died the following day. He was eighty-one years old.[22]

Billy Joe Shaver never did find the recognition he deserved throughout the course of his life, a fact that he acknowledged years prior, as he pointed to his still-outstanding induction into the Country Music Hall of Fame. "If you don't want to put me in there, that's fine," Shaver told *Rolling Stone* in 2014. "But I just don't understand it to tell you the truth. I feel like I am part of the foundation and maybe even a cornerstone. I think I'm that much."[23]

Hard to Be an Outlaw

Rodney Crowell

The outlaw movement of the seventies wouldn't have happened without "Ride Me Down Easy" or "Georgia on a Fast Train." Billy Joe laid it out there for people to understand. The movement was driven by language

Rodney Crowell, Telluride Bluegrass Festival, Telluride, Colorado, June 20, 2004. Photo by Brian T. Atkinson.

and attitude. He had an individualistic, rugged persona. He's a blustery, larger-than-life Texan, and that culture manifests in his self-expression. Billy Joe can be scary when he performs. You don't know which way it's going to go. He's enigmatic and compelling, much in the way Guy Clark was. What you see is what you get.

Johnny Cash played "I'm Just an Old Chunk of Coal" for me the first time I heard it. I recognized Billy Joe's writing was real right away. He's a poet, vulnerable and sincere. He opens his coat and shows his heart in a way that's evocative and beautiful. That's high regard from where I sit. You have to have poetry in your blood to earn rank with Bob Dylan or Guy Clark. Billy Joe has it in spades. Billy Joe said of Guy Clark during a conversation, "It's like I'm sitting at a bus stop, waiting for a train." I said, "That's a good line. Can I steal it from you?" "Yeah, I'll never use it." It became the opening line of "It Ain't over Yet," the song I wrote about Guy. Billy Joe has always been thoughtful and kind-hearted. He's irrepressible, but there's a sweet soul underneath.[1]

Rodney Crowell, born August 7, 1950, in Houston, Texas, found commercial success with the release of his 1988 album Diamonds and Dirt, *which included five number-one songs, such as "After All This Time," "I Couldn't Leave You if I Tried," and the Guy Clark co-write "She's Crazy for Leaving." His 2017 release* Close Ties *features the Grammy-winning song "It Ain't over Yet," a collaboration with ex-wife Rosanne Cash and Grammy winner John Paul White (the Civil Wars). He is the author of* Chinaberry Sidewalks: A Memoir, *published in 2012.*

Bobby Bare Jr.

I first met Billy Joe Shaver in 1971. He used to hang out in my dad's office. I was busy being a kid, so I wasn't there all the time. My dad did him a favor [signing him to a publishing deal]. He used to own Billy Joe's first batch of songs, which included everything on *Honky Tonk Heroes*. "Ride Me Down Easy" has always been a big part of my dad's show. I love it. I've never seen a show where he didn't play it.

I really got to know Billy Joe as an adult. He came to see my show at the Troubadour in Los Angeles, California, when I was with my first rock band. I didn't know he was there. "I came in and saw you play," he told

Bobby Bare Jr. Photo by Joshua Black Wilkins, courtesy of Bloodshot Records.

me years later. "That was awful, godawful." Then he told me he loved my new singer-songwriter solo stuff that wasn't crazy, loud rock. He's unpredictable. I went to see him play at a club in Austin, Texas. He said, "Man, now follow me. Follow me." He walked up onstage, "Ladies and gentlemen, this is Bobby Bare Jr. He's going to sing a couple of songs for you." I flew all the way to Austin to sing background vocals for him at Willie's Picnic. Just as we were about to walk out there, he said, "Don't come out. Don't sing." He just wasn't feeling it at that moment. He's the opposite of most young guys in Nashville who worry about what pickup they're going to put in their acoustic guitar. He walks around with his miniature guitar and doesn't even plug it in. He's all heart.

Also, Billy Joe is fearless. He lets his character show. He's a great performer in the same way as my dad. He [focuses on] his lyrics and storytelling. He has a great sense of observation and flow. He sees things, sticks them in a song, and turns it into great poetry. He's always excited to talk about his songs. He still has that level of feeling. The desire to write good songs is burning in him and hits you. He's such a tough guy, yet he's vulnerable and absolutely loveable. [Then] he'll turn on a dime. When he gets mad, he's scary, horrifying, and dangerous. He's extreme Texas.[2]

Bobby Bare Jr., born June 28, 1966, in Nashville, is the son of country music legend Bobby Bare. He received a Grammy nomination at age six for his collaboration with his father on the Shel Silverstein–penned "Daddy, What if . . .?" Bare Jr. recorded two albums with his hard rock band called Bare Jr. (Boo-tay *in 1998 and* Brainwasher *in 2000) before signing with Bloodshot Records as a solo artist in 2002. He is currently a member of the indie rock band Guided by Voices.*

Harold F. Eggers Jr.

I started out as Townes [Van Zandt]'s road manager in 1977. He took me under his wing. Everywhere he went, I went with him.

Townes had an ability to know someone's demons. He used to warn me about Billy Joe. "Harold, be careful with him. He can go quickly from Bible thumping to beating you up. Keep a distance in case some-

Left to right: Townes Van Zandt and Harold F. Eggers Jr. at Pedernales Recording Studio near Austin, Texas. Photo courtesy of Harold F. Eggers Jr.

one says something that rears him up." The first time I met Billy Joe, he shook my hand, and rubbed his half finger in my palm. I pulled it back and wiped it off: "Gee, what was that?" Billy Joe reared back to hit me. Townes stepped in and said, "Hold it, Billy Joe. He's with me. Leave Harold alone." Billy Joe put his hand out and said, "Okay, Townes."

When I moved to Nashville, I was staying at Townes's cabin, which was more like a shanty. There was running water, but it was from a well, so we used to go to John Lomax III's house to take showers every three days. Billy Joe came out with all these characters on motorcycles. They would go to the bars, and I would sit off to the side and hear them joking about their days in Houston and how wild they would get taking acid and drinking. Billy Joe said in Brian T. Atkinson's book [*I'll Be Here in the Morning: The Songwriting Legacy of Townes Van Zandt*] that he and Townes would go on a tear in Houston, and people would try to rob them, and they'd get in fights, beating up six or seven people at a time. Billy Joe tried to blame it on Townes. I always knew Townes was dangerous, but I never saw it physically. Townes was dangerous with words, but reading what Billy Joe said, I guess Townes must have been dangerous physically. When you shook his hand, you could tell how strong he was. Now that I look back, I remember Townes used to say to me, "Harold, you don't understand. This is dangerous." "What are you talking about, Townes? You go from town to town and meet girls. What a life." "No, no, no, Harold. You don't realize. We go to these places, and there are jealous husbands, jealous boyfriends. There's guns and knives. You can get killed." The lives they lived were extremely dangerous. They were modern-day outlaws, and their guns were their guitars.

In 1977, I saw Billy Joe nearly kill [fiddle player] Owen Cody at the Gold Rush bar in Nashville. We were sitting at a front booth catching up on local music. Billy Joe said he was going to remarry his ex-wife, Brenda. Townes said, "That's great, Billy Joe." Cody laughed, "Why are you marrying that fat cow again?" Billy Joe's eyes bulged, his face turned red, and he grabbed Cody, punching him in the head. Blood was gushing out. Then he dragged him out the door and to the sidewalk and slammed him against a parked car. He raised him in the air, swung him down, banging his head against the wheel cap. Townes ran out, "Stop, Billy Joe. You're killing him." Billy Joe seemed like he didn't hear him. We were trying to figure out if Cody was still alive. Then Billy says to Townes,

"Do you need a fiddle player?" "I guess I do now." Billy dropped Cody, "He's all yours." Cody was in the band from that point on.[3] Billy Joe was just so rough. He almost killed him.

There was a time when [legendary Bob Dylan and Johnny Cash producer] Bob Johnston was producing Billy Joe, and Bob had on this Native American necklace. Billy Joe says, "Hey, Bob, can I wear it while I'm recording?" "Okay." Billy Joe didn't want to give it back. Finally, Bob told him, "Billy Joe, I'm going outside. I will have a two-by-four, and you won't know it, but when you come out, I'll knock you out, man." Well, Billy Joe gave it back to him.

Townes did some dates up north in Vermont and Massachusetts with Billy Joe. Townes very rarely picked up his guitar. He'd only play it at gigs. I'd say, "Townes, why don't you keep your chops up by playing? These other guys do it. Aren't you worried that God's going to take the gift away from you because you're not respecting it?" He'd get mad at me and say, "No, Harold. You don't understand. I practice when I do my first song [onstage]." Even in the cabin, I never saw him pull out the guitar, but we were staying at this farm, and Billy would sing, and then pass the guitar to Townes. There was another time in Santa Fe with Guy Clark and Billy [when] they passed the guitar around. It was rare and very special. Townes and Billy Joe caused chaos, but they watched out for one another. When Brenda came down with cancer, Townes said she was going to die and talked about her in a loving way. These guys were notorious, but they really cared about each other.[4]

Harold F. Eggers Jr. is an Austin, Texas-based music industry executive with forty years' experience. He met Townes Van Zandt in 1967 when Van Zandt was signed to Kevin Eggers's Poppy Records (later Tomato Records), which released the bulk of Van Zandt's work, beginning with his 1968 debut, For the Sake of the Song. *Eggers went to work as Van Zandt's road manager in 1977 and was with him up until his death on January 1, 1997. He is the author of the 2017 memoir,* My Years with Townes Van Zandt: Music, Genius, and Rage *(Backbeat Books).*

Billy Don Burns

I moved to Nashville in 1972. After I was there about a month, Harlan Howard signed me as a writer with his company, Wilderness Music. Waylon hung out there, and Billy Joe came through. He's just a good ole country boy who brought his music to the city. Billy Joe saw me kick the dog shit out of old Tompall Glaser when that album [*Wanted! The Outlaws]* hi*t [in 1976] with Waylon, Willie, Jessi [Colter], and Tompall. Tompall's head got real big. He thought he was badass. I saw him cuss out people like dogs. I thought, *Man, if he ever does that to me? We're going to go in the street.* Sure enough, my buddy Ken McDuffy called me, and said "Tompall's cutting an album and he'll cut a song with you."

We went down to Tompall's [Hillbilly Central] studio in Nashville, and Tompall came out with Captain Midnight. We told him we wanted to play him a song. Tompall said, Let's go have a cocktail first. We went

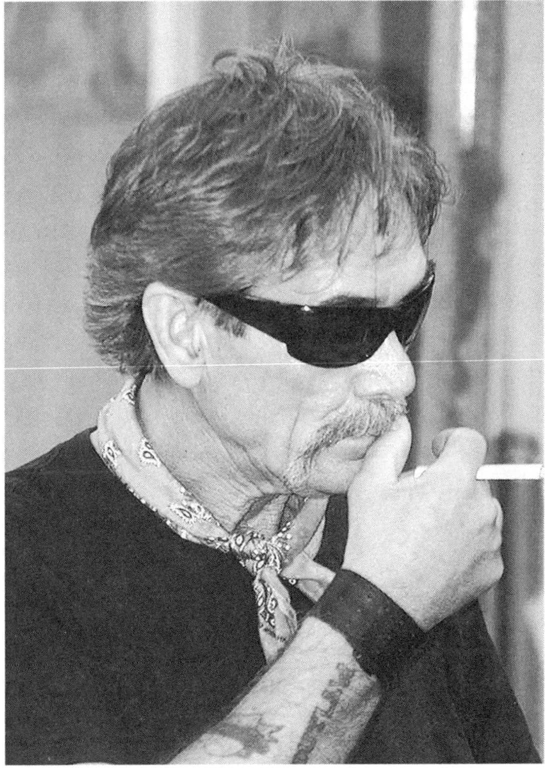

Billy Don Burns. Photo by Debra Williams.

down the street to a place called Third Coast. Tompall said, "I guess I gotta pay for the drinks since I'm the only millionaire in the bunch." I said, "Tompall, you ought to get on your hands and knees every day of your life and kiss Waylon's ass for giving you a ride on that *Outlaw* album." He jumped on me, and I put the leather to him. My buddy had to pull me off. When I saw Waylon, he said, "I don't know what he done, but I'm sure he deserved it." I said, "He didn't have no other way, Waylon." Billy Joe was there, and [years later] he wrote the liner notes for my album *Nights When I'm Sober: Portrait of a Honky Tonk* and said, "[Billy Don] is the best man to have on your side no matter how dangerous the situation."

We played three days in Huntsville, Alabama, back in 1990. Billy met this waitress [Jean] and married her the next day. We had a party at a bar, and everybody was drinking and having fun. Eddy was still alive. He was really hot then. He had one of those [wireless] transformers on his guitar and went table to table to speak and play the hell out of the Stratocaster. [Jean] was around Eddy's age. He [jokingly] called her Mama. It was wild, and the marriage was short-lived.

We were friends with Sergeant Barry Sadler, who had a monster hit with "Ballad of the Green Berets." It topped all the charts and passed the Beatles to get to number one. As a professional soldier, he was always going somewhere to train. He went to Guatemala to train the Contras and was shot by an assassin. They flew him back to Nashville. Me, Billy Joe, and Billy Ray Reynolds, who played guitar for Waylon, went to see him at the Veterans [Administration] hospital. He had a big canal through his head and died the next day. It was heavy.[5]

Billy Don Burns, born in Arkansas, is an outlaw country artist who moved in 1972 to Nashville, where he landed his first publishing deal with Wilderness Music. Burns performed as Hank Williams Sr. at Opryland USA in 1973, and that year his song "Be Alright in Arkansas" was recorded by Connie Smith and "I'll Always Come Back Loving You" by Mel Tillis. He released his critically acclaimed debut album Long Lost Highway *in 1990 and collaborated with Hank Cochran on the album* Desperate Men *in 1996. In 2002, he released his second solo album,* Train Called Lonesome.

Ray Wylie Hubbard

I discovered Billy Joe Shaver before I discovered his music. Back in the early seventies, we used to play Mother Blues in Dallas, Texas. Bill Simonson ran it and said one night, "Come over here. I want you to meet this songwriter named Billy Joe Shaver. He's incredible." I went over to the table where Billy Joe was sitting. Bill introduced us, "Billy Joe, this is Ray Wylie Hubbard. Ray Wylie, this is Billy Joe Shaver." Billy Joe looks up and says, "I just took some LSD about two hours ago, and I need another half inch." "What?" He held his finger, thumb and finger up and said, "I just need another half inch." I knew I was going to like him off the bat.

I heard he was playing the Dripping Springs Picnic with Willie Nelson later. [Nelson's legendary harmonica player] Mickey Raphael told me about it. That's where I really got into him. Billy was there at the start of

Ray Wylie Hubbard on his back porch, Wimberley, Texas, November 14, 2017. Photo by Brian T. Atkinson.

the outlaw movement. He was ornery before Waylon Jennings was. He had shaggy hair before Willie grew out his. He may not have invented the movement, but he brought the cool outlaw vibe to it. He's not going to let people tell him what to write, how to sing, or how to act. He was instrumental in putting forth that attitude for everyone else. I admire the fact that he does whatever the hell he wants. That's what the outlaw movement was based on. He's fearless as a writer and a performer. "Black Rose" from *Honky Tonk Heroes* shows you how fearless he is. That song crossed a [color] barrier that hadn't been crossed before.

Billy Joe and I have never written together. I've done collaborations with other people, but there's this quote by Roger Miller, "Writing is like an old cat having kittens, she just crawls under the porch herself and has kittens." I look at songwriting as a solo thing. Billy has done the same. He has collaborated on songs, but for the most part he writes independently. Texans have a real sense of independence that carries over to songwriting. We were our own country for a while. Billy Joe embodies this incredible pride from the history of Texas, with the Alamo, to Sam Houston. He's written songs covered by artists from [Elvis] to Waylon Jennings, but he isn't writing because he has to give some publisher twelve songs a year. He's not writing songs to try to get Tim McGraw to record them. He's writing songs thinking about their future, being in the moment of writing that song. That's how it's done right. It makes me want to be a better writer when I hear Billy Joe's songs because he sets the bar so high. I try to achieve that when I write, but I'm not sure if I'll ever get there.

His performances are powerful, like watching a spiritual wrestling match. He gets the crowd fired up and excited. He's had way too much tragedy in his life, so for him get on a stage and make people feel good, whoop, holler, dance, and yell says a lot about his courage. You're drawn to him. He'll be full-tilt outlaw, and then, the next minute, he'll get down on a knee, take his hat off, and pray. Then he gets back up and roars. That's Billy Joe Shaver. He's mesmerizing. You don't take your eyes off him.

Whenever we'd do a gig together his name on the marquee would be in two-inch letters and "Ray Wylie Hubbard" is in one-inch letters, but Billy Joe will call me up and go, "Ray, I'm older than you, I'm going to go on first." "What? No. You're Billy Joe Shaver. You're the headliner."

"I'm going on first. I won't be long." He's always been supportive and encouraging. He'll walk by when I'm onstage and say, "Give 'em hell, Ray." Then the next time he walks by he'll say, "I'm prayin' for ya, Ray." He's always treated me with kindness and respect. There's no ego, no diva about him. He's written phenomenal songs, yet there's great humility about him. I adore him as an artist and as a man. He's a standup guy, and I have a feeling that if I ever needed anything, I could call him up and he'd be there for me.

I can't wait to hear his new record every time he puts one out because I know it will be significant. Those are the songs he writes. They're significant poetry but down-to-earth. If Rimbaud had a guitar, it would be like Billy Joe Shaver. There's also this Walt Whitman quality to his songs. They hold a lot of depth, but he writes with a basic humanity, and he's able to put it in everyday language. He writes from a place where the true poet lives.

There's a bunch of goobers with guitars running around saying they're songwriters, but Billy Joe is real, not some manufactured fake guy. Guy Clark, Townes Van Zandt, and Billy Joe Shaver are the three guys who form the Holy Trinity of Texas songwriters. Those are the guys Texas songwriters aspire to be. Those are the guys you want to study and listen to, to be that writer. You want to try to have songs that have that depth and weight. That's going to be Billy Joe's legacy.[6]

Ray Wylie Hubbard, born November 13, 1946, in Soper, Oklahoma, is a Texas-based singer-songwriter whose career spans five decades. Hubbard came to prominence when Jerry Jeff Walker recorded the song "Redneck Mother" on his 1973 album ¡Viva Terlingua! *A self-proclaimed "spiritual mongrel," Hubbard achieved sobriety on his forty-first birthday, inspired by fellow Texan Stevie Ray Vaughan. He has since gone through a spiritual awakening that is reflected in his heavily blues-influenced songwriting. In 2017, he released the single "Tell the Devil . . . I'm Getting There as Fast as I Can," a collaboration with Lucinda Williams that appears on Hubbard's album of the same name. Hubbard took home the Outlaw Male honor at the 2019 Ameripolitan Awards. He is the subject of the recent Texas A&M University Press book* The Messenger: The Songwriting Legacy of Ray Wylie Hubbard, *by Brian T. Atkinson.*

Lee Roy Parnell

Billy Joe Shaver, Townes Van Zandt, and Guy Clark were all going way deeper than the rest of us. If you look at them as a trilogy, you wonder who the prince would be. I think Guy. He was prince-like. He was also rough as a cop. Townes was the jester. Billy Joe was the most natural. He['s] pure Corsicana, black-dirt genius. God just spit him out to do this exact thing that he's doing. He was born into a horrific situation, and the country changed vastly during his formative years. If you look deep enough, you can't separate his music from his life. He's heartfelt and wide open all the time. His songwriting set the bar and made everybody else better.

The last time Billy Joe lived in Nashville, he lived in an apartment in Bellevue not far from where I lived. I reached out and asked if he'd like to write for an afternoon, and he took me up on it. We sat at the kitchen table with two guitars, spending the afternoon writing. It was so enjoyable. We laughed hard. I wish we had more of those days.

Billy Joe is as strong physically as he is mentally. He has two speeds—on and off. You never know what's going to happen. He's the toughest man I've known, and, on my best day, I would not take him on. What's wrong with music these days is that the danger is gone. Social media is a wonderful tool, but what made rock and roll and country cool was the mystique. We've sold it at a merch table and lost it. With Billy Joe Shaver, there's no chance of that. He's living out there by himself, fearless, with a sharp wit. They're not making them like that anymore. He will remain unchanged. He's like no other human being.[7]

Lee Roy Parnell, born in Stephenville, Texas, on December 21, 1965, is a country and blues singer-songwriter. Parnell moved to Nashville in 1987 and has released nine studio albums, starting with his 1990 Arista Records self-titled debut. He has had over twenty songs land on Billboard's Hot Country Songs chart (with "What Kind of Fool Do You Think I Am," "Tender Moment," and "A Little Bit You" reaching number two).

Lee Roy Parnell promotional poster. Photo of poster by Courtney S. Lennon.

Steve Earle

I first discovered Billy Joe in the seventies growing up in Texas. I was fifteen and had been playing music for a little while in coffeehouses because I was too young to play places that served liquor. Willie Nelson moved back to Texas around that time, and that's when Armadillo World Headquarters [opened]. I used to go [from San Antonio] to Austin to see shows there. I think the first time I remember actually seeing Billy Joe was at the [Dripping Springs Reunion in 1971], which was the precursor to [Willie Nelson's Fourth of July] Picnic. Willie didn't put it on, but he played it and was the headliner. There were actually bigger acts, but Willie was the big local act. Billy Joe was on it. I'd moved to Houston by that time, so I knew [Columbia Records artist] Danny Epps. He was there to play with Billy and missed his set because he was puffing a joint with me.

Steve Earle, Austin City Limits Music Festival, Austin, Texas, October 13, 2012. Photo by Brian T. Atkinson.

I think Billy Joe and I probably met at Guy and Susanna [Clark]'s house. He always knew who I was from that point on. I was always very proud of that. I bought his first record when it came out. Billy's always been a big deal to me. He and Mickey Newbury are two people I met really young who seemed to know I was real. Texas has more than its share of great songwriters. Newbury was the godfather. He got there first. He discovered Townes and was his first publisher. It took me a long time to get a record deal. Just those guys knowing me and coming across the room to say hi to me was a big deal and kept me going for years. It was always an honor that he knew who I was.

I know no one else that came from the background [Billy Joe] did [who] wasn't a hipster because Guy, Townes, and me were. I just thought he was like Willie and Kris and a few others [who] were a little more cerebral than some country artists, but there's a big difference: Billy Joe's not a post–Bob Dylan songwriter. I don't think he knew who Bob Dylan was when he started writing songs. Kris was playing folk festivals and definitely knew who Bob Dylan was. I wrote liner notes for Billy Joe's [*Long in the Tooth*] album and said, "Most of us, the generation of writers who arrived in Nashville a step or two behind Billy Joe were either post-Dylan folkies angling for a songwriter draw or semi-enlightened hillbillies striving to reach a next level of artistry."[8]

As I started writing better and studying where [music] comes from, I figured out Billy Joe was a supernaturally literate songwriter. There's nothing to explain in his education. He's read stuff. I'm not even sure what, but he came with this natural sense of metaphor. Nobody taught him. He could naturally alliterate like great writers do. I was using internal rhymes and alliteration before I knew I was doing it. My education got through the eighth grade, but I would always come to some point where I'd realize there was something I didn't know and go back and try to learn it myself. So I've read everything William Shakespeare's ever written, everything Ernest Hemingway has ever written, and everything that J. K. Rowling has ever written. I assume Billy Joe did, but I never witnessed it. I saw Townes read. That's all he did.

Billy Joe's just always been one of my favorite writers who I can go back to learn from, [yet] I've still never been able to come up with an explanation for why he is the way he is. He writes in vernacular, but he also has a formal language. I know his formal language comes from the Bible. Mine comes from the Bible and Shakespeare. Same with Townes. It's strange because my spiritual system is pretty distant from him. I believe in God, but I'm not a Christian. Billy Joe is, but he's one of a handful of Christians I'm personally acquainted with who are into God and not hurting anybody in the process. A sentence like "Lest I should become vain along the way" is straight out of the Bible. We covered "Ain't No God in Mexico" on my record [*So You Wanna Be an Outlaw*] as a bonus track with the line, "Pity me, I didn't find the line in time." Sometimes you've got to abandon [writing] the way you talk to say certain things at certain times.

Billy Joe doesn't give a fuck [when he performs]. He has obvious physical things to overcome to play guitar and be a singer-songwriter. He always felt like he needed a band because of his lack of digits. So I've never seen him solo. Early on he always had Danny Epps or somebody playing along with him. Then he had Eddy until he was gone. Back in 1987, there was a time I saw Billy Joe [where] Eddy had put together a particularly bad band, and the songs went horribly off the rails. I was sitting front row, so I heard it. Billy Joe just turned around, walked past Eddy, and said, "Shoot that monkey!" He went off and back on, laughing. It wasn't about Eddy. He loved him. He was hard on him, but his delivery is straight ahead and patterned after old school country acting.

I was in England producing a record [for] a band called the Bible in late 1987 and writing songs for *Copperhead Road*, getting ready to record it. I came home, and there was a stack of mail under the door. I was going through a divorce and living in [an] apartment. I was running through my messages. There was one from Billy Joe saying, "Steve, this is Billy Joe. I just want to let you know, Eddy's ready to come on over and play on that record you're getting ready to make in Memphis." I hadn't asked Eddy to come over and play on the record. The guitar player I had was gone, but I'd already replaced him with Webb Wilder's guitarist Donny Roberts, who was always going to be the guitar player on that record. I tracked Eddy down and said, "Hey man. I'm sorry, but your dad must have said something that gave you the wrong impression. I don't need a guitar player." Eddy was a great guitar player, but I watched him feuding with his dad, and I didn't want any part of it.

I don't think [Billy Joe] ever thought about being an outlaw. I don't think any of us did. [Publicist Hazel Smith] made that term up. I like a little guilt in my drinking song. We were unapologetic about that on some levels, but we also knew we were wrong. Billy constantly had this methodology that I think all of us emulated—finding a way to look at the worst things about ourselves and make it poetic. Billy Joe had this unique position that he sat in and looked at himself and looked at us. He managed to write songs [like] "Willy the Wandering Gypsy and Me" that were about his friends and people that he knew, but he knew how to keep them universal so anybody [could] relate to it. When David Allan Coe did it, it wasn't the same thing. He just didn't get it, but Billy Joe [did]. He mostly [looked] at himself. I have had girls argue about which song of mine is about her, and the truth is they are all about me when you get right down to it. Any good writer wrote their songs all about themselves.

Outlaw artists were country artists that had come from country music, country people, but they were smarter and more progressive as musicians and songwriters. So they had trouble. Willie failed as a country singer and moved back to Texas. Billy Joe was hardheaded about holding Waylon Jennings to his promise. I've heard [the *Honky Tonk Heroes*] story from Billy Joe, Waylon, and from Jessi since. The truth is not exactly how Billy Joe tells it. Nothing nefarious about it. Billy Joe was not exactly sober. These stories grow when you tell them. Some of the best rumors of me out there, I made up myself, and I don't know which ones are true or not. Waylon was more successful and really chomping at the bit. That moment comes along and here comes Billy Joe Shaver, and Waylon makes that one record that defines outlaw country if there is such a thing. When Waylon decided, "No, I'm going to produce my own record," it happens to be a record of Billy Joe Shaver songs. Billy Joe made sure those songs got heard. He was determined that something was going to be and tried to will it into existence. *Honky Tonk Heroes* was a masterpiece.[9]

Steve Earle, born January 17, 1955, in Fort Monroe, Virginia, but raised near San Antonio in Schertz, Texas, dropped out of school in 1973 and began following his idol Townes Van Zandt around the coffeehouse folk music circuit. He arrived in Nashville in the mid-seventies and became a member of Guy Clark's band, playing bass on Clark's 1975 debut, Old No 1. *Earle made a name for himself in the mid-eighties, rising to prominence with a country-rock style that led to crossover success with songs like "Guitar Town," "Someday," and "Copperhead Road." He produced a stunning three-album run after beating addiction and emerging from jail time with* Train A-Comin' *(1995),* I Feel Alright *(1996), and* El Corazon *(1997).*

Honky Tonk Heroes

Jessi Colter

The first time I met Billy Joe Shaver was in the early seventies. We met him when Waylon and I were touring. We were staying at a hotel down on Nineteenth Avenue in Nashville. Billy came to the door and was bringing some tapes for Waylon. I usually never answered the door. It's just what you learn to do as a celebrity. Billy Joe was standing outside the door and said, "I have some tapes I'd like to give to Waylon." I opened the door and took the tapes from him. I was protective of our privacy, but there was something about Billy Joe. He had a great humility about him. He's a big guy, but he doesn't have the you-better-listen-to-me attitude. I know he speaks of times [when] he and Waylon had a run-in, but I opened the door because he was genuine. He was really nervous and won my heart. I took the tapes from him, and Waylon seemed like he was interested, which he rarely was. I can't remember if any of the songs wound up on *Honky Tonk Heroes*. Billy Joe probably doesn't even know. The only person who would is Waylon.

I couldn't believe the way they treated artists when I first got to Nashville with Waylon. I had been with Duane Eddy in the rock field and saw how people treated entertainers. They handed them a big $250,000 check and let them do whatever they wanted. Not in Nashville. They were going to squeeze every dollar and put it in their own pocket. Waylon wasn't really appreciated in those days in Nashville. People loved him from the time he came out in 1966, but when I saw what he was going through creatively, I thought, *This is really crazy.* They made Waylon sound like

Jessi Colter, 1975 *Billboard* advertisement. Photo of original by Courtney S. Lennon.

he was crazy. Waylon was basically producing his own music at the time they started *Honky Tonk Heroes*, except he wasn't running the board, and he used their engineer. There was a lot of conflict around getting the album done. It was a challenging time. Waylon had been through so much with the moving producers at RCA running in the horns on a beautifully produced record. Waylon governed a lot in those days, even with producers.

I was delighted when he decided to do *Honky Tonk Heroes*. I was in and out of the studio when they were recording it. They started recording after he fired everyone and took over. Richie Albright [drummer for Jennings's band the Waylors] and Waylon were trying to figure out the technical part of running the board. Danny Davis ran in as a substitute producer. He had these ideas that were nothing like Waylon's. Waylon finally asked him to leave. He'd come to [the end of] his rope. It wasn't because Waylon was spoiled or a hothead. Of course, Waylon got annoyed by Billy Joe coming into the session and telling him what to do. That didn't work.

Honky Tonk Heroes broke new ground. [The album is] great American music and put Billy Joe on the map. I loved it immediately when the album was done. The songs are great, Texas-primitive, genuine. *Honky Tonk Heroes* became a remarkable milestone and is to this day music about the working man, the man who hasn't had it easy and has had to scrap for a living. Waylon loved doing those songs. Waylon got into Billy Joe because he would scrap. Billy Joe didn't really know how to act when Waylon first cut his songs. Waylon fixed that.

I'd see Billy Joe after he'd had a big fight in an alley. I knew he was a scrapper. He could be easily fired up especially if he was drinking, but I didn't see that part of him. Billy Joe was always cool around me. He didn't pull a lot of punches. I remember Bobby Duvall talking about him later because he saw the man side of Billy Joe. I never did.

I always try to see Billy Joe whenever I know he's going to be performing. He beats all I've ever seen as a performer because he's a writer, and he's a talker. He gives it everything he's got when he gets up there. I saw him about three weeks after he had a knee replacement, and it killed me. He was getting in this van riding to the next date, and he was apologizing for not being able to dance too good onstage. I about cried. I talked to him several times when I heard he was in trouble and had heart surgery. I called him and said, "Who's taking care of you?" He said, "I am."

He was supposed to be on the Outlaw Country Cruise with me in 2016, but he stopped at the bank and said he wasn't coming on, even though he was supposed to have a big interview with Steve Earle for Sirius XM. He decided not to come. He does things like that. One time he called and asked me if I'd sing on something. I said yes, but I never heard back from him. Everybody knows he pretty much does what he wants to.

During the outlaw movement in the early seventies, we were all just trying to stay alive. Waylon had health issues at points, but that isn't why this happened. Billy Joe just came up to me and said, "I'm gonna pray for you." I'll never forget it. It came at a time when it meant a lot because no one said that back in those days. I love Billy Joe. We built a friendship throughout the years. He's defiantly a Texas boy. He's a handful, to say it mildly, but I can handle him. He gets a little out of line or out there, and I either laugh it off or straighten it up. He's an original, not the norm. He's very energetic and has his ways. You have to lean back, relax, and enjoy him. Billy's a unique original American and Texan.[1]

Jessi Colter, born Miriam Johnson, May 25, 1943, in Phoenix, Arizona, was discovered by rock guitarist Duane Eddy who produced her first single, "Lonesome Road," 1961. Colter married Eddy in 1962, and the couple moved to California. After their divorce in 1968, Colter returned to Phoenix and met country legend Waylon Jennings, who she married in 1969. Jennings produced her 1970 debut A Country Star Is Born, *and her 1976* I'm Jessi Colter *featured the number-one hit "I'm Not Lisa," which was nominated for a Grammy. Colter appeared alongside Jennings, Willie Nelson, and Tompall Glaser on the 1975 platinum country album* Wanted! The Outlaws. *Her 1981 self-penned duet with Waylon Jennings "Storms Never Last" went to number seventeen on the charts. She was married to Jennings until his death on February 13, 2002. The couple had one child together, Outlaw Country artist Shooter Jennings.*

Ray Benson (Asleep at the Wheel)

Billy Joe is right up there with Willie Nelson, Waylon Jennings, Jerry Jeff Walker, and Guy Clark. That bunch is high cotton, and Billy Joe absolutely holds his own. He's as amazing as his songs. He was the songster of the outlaw movement. We'd call him our "right-hand man," because he only had three fingers. *Honky Tonk Heroes* was the definition of outlaw, and the way he got it done was the definition of outlaw. He threatened Waylon.

I first met Billy Joe in 1973 at a big concert in Terlingua, Texas. Willie, Waylon, Billy Joe, Jerry Jeff Walker, and Asleep at the Wheel were on the bill. After we played, Billy Joe came up to me. I had never met the guy. He said, "I'm really disappointed in you." "Why's that?" "I heard you were just like Bob Wills. You don't drop meter." "Well, I [won't] now, Billy Joe." In schooled musicians, dropping meter means counting time. Bob Wills didn't drop meter because he didn't read music. He came in when he wanted. Billy Joe does the same. It was revealing. He had great

Ray Benson, backstage at Austin City Limits Music Festival, Austin, Texas, October 8, 2010. Photo by Brian T. Atkinson

perception powers. That's what a songwriter is, somebody who sees and makes the world work. I love Billy Joe's songwriting, and the way he looks at life. He's a true poet who harkens back to some of the great musical forms. If you listen to "Honky Tonk Heroes," it's classic ragtime, but he doesn't know that. He just knows what he knows.

In the seventies, we were all coming from very diverse places: Billy Joe in Waco, Jerry Jeff in New York, Guy Clark in South Texas, and me in Pennsylvania. We were trying to make it in this business that was so different from where we were in country, which was straight Nashville 1960s as opposed to the outlaw movement. We were breaking musical laws. It was all based on not wanting to be told what to do by the Nashville establishment. The reason we were outlaws is because we did drugs, and drugs were illegal. We all had our favorites. Willie and I had pot. Waylon had cocaine, which almost killed him. After we quit hard drugs, Bonnie Raitt said, "There was a lot of bad stuff, but there was a lot of really good stuff." There were jam sessions that were legendary because we all stayed up late. Billy Joe was wild as they come. He drank. We all did, but he paid the price for it more so than others and did a lot of damage to himself and his family. He was married and divorced I don't know how many times. His son was such a great guitar player, but Billy led him down the wrong path. It was so sad. He changed big time after those events, especially Eddy's passing. He got real religious. I've never seen anyone get the kind of religion he got. He's best friends with Kinky Friedman, and yet he sings this great line, "If you don't love Jesus, go to Hell."

I'm one of the first that had a single with a Billy Joe song, with "Way Down Texas Way" in 1987. It was top forty on the country charts. Willie's nephew Freddy Fletcher played drums for him and suggested I do it. It's a great song. We did our first video ever. It was before they put country acts in videos. It's a two-step number, and we'd do it every night at a dance hall. I was talking to Gary Nicholson, who wrote [several] songs with Billy Joe, and said, "You never know what's going to come out of Billy Joe's mouth." He's very unpredictable. I love him dearly. I think the world of him and am glad we're friends, but I don't see him a lot. We played with him last year in Kerrville, Texas, for Kinky Friedman's dog rescue. He was great. He's getting old and has some health problems, but he's an amazing guy. He had a deadbeat dad, a tough life, and great faith he believes to the core. In the seventies, Asleep at the Wheel did "I Been to Georgia on a Fast Train." I remember him coming up and singing that with us. Then I remember another time when he came up to me drunk as shit, falling all over himself. That was seventies Billy Joe. I know he shot the guy in Lorena, but he's really mellowed out.[2]

Ray Benson, born March 16, 1951, in Philadelphia, Pennsylvania, is the front man for the multi-Grammy-winning western swing group Asleep at the Wheel. Benson is also an accomplished producer whose credits include Suzy Bogguss, Aaron Watson, James Hand, and Carolyn Wonderland. Benson teamed up with honky-tonker Dale Watson on the 2016 album Dale & Ray, *which included the song "Feelin' Haggard," a tribute to the late Merle Haggard.*

Kinky Friedman

Things came to flashpoint in Nashville with *Honky Tonk Heroes*. That's when Waylon gave Captain Midnight one hundred dollars to keep Billy Joe out of the studio. Waylon had these Hell's Angels bodyguards, but Billy Joe would have been a match for anybody. Midnight gave Billy Joe the money, and Billy Joe threw it back at Midnight and said, "Tell

Kinky Friedman, Buffalo Iron Works, Buffalo, New York, July 8, 2018. Photo by Mark Whitfield Lennon.

Waylon to stick this up his ass." Midnight was a very special person and very close to Billy Joe and me, but we don't know if Waylon stuck it up his ass or not. History doesn't tell us if it got that high up the food chain. In Waylon's defense, if you get a chance to record a record, and you wrote the fucking song, I don't really want your ass around when I'm singing it. Especially if you're commenting and critiquing all the time, which Billy Joe was, but that record came out great. It's the only one of its kind. A country boy stumbles into a studio. That's what Nashville should be all about.

I have to be in a very miserable and tragic mood to write. Anybody does. You're not going to write a great song if you're not miserable. Billy Joe comes by it honestly. He's had a shitload of tragedy in his life, and everybody in his family is just about gone. His childhood in Corsicana was dreadful, [yet] his songs uplifted millions of people. Billy Joe and Willie Nelson both struggled with failure and success, but Willie was a guy who didn't think twice about leaving his wife and kids in poverty. I don't think Billy Joe would ever do that. Willie was a scoundrel, but he was struggling to get by and was later remorseful about it. Nobody understood what Willie was doing, even after he'd already had hit songs for other people like "Hello Walls" [which Faron Young took to number one in 1961].

When Willie left Nashville for Texas in 1971, no one thought they would see or hear about him again. They didn't hate him, but Chet Atkins had all the power, and he never did anything for Willie except put him in a fucking sweater. Nashville dropped the ball on Willie— and Hank Williams. You can't blame everything on Nashville, but it was a town without pity that didn't nurture the two biggest superstars in the whole fucking universe of country music.

Billy Joe is a songwriter's songwriter, which means they don't like him. They don't think it's commercial, when in truth he's very commercial. If he had somebody handling his career early on, he would have a hell of a lot of money from songs recorded by everybody from Elvis to Bob Dylan, but that's not what he's like. He doesn't have a team of lawyers working for him. He quickly burns through agents and managers. I'm on his side. It's not a great thing to have a Colonel Tom Parker type of manager. Elvis wouldn't have been a superstar without Colonel Tom, but he might have been a human being who lived a fucking life. Billy was always at the opposite end of bad publishing deals, jumping labels, with no one appreciating him. That's the thing with publishing. Those songs are worth a fucking bundle, and Billy Joe can't do anything. It's unthinkable. Willie can call his lawyers and see if there's some money rattling around, and they'll come up with a million bucks that was being held onto by some fucker. Billy Joe ought to be able to do that, but he can't.

[John] Steinbeck told Woody Guthrie he was very jealous of the fact that he spent ten years writing *The Grapes of Wrath*, and Woody got the character Tom Joad down in ten minutes in a song better than Steinbeck did with his big Tom Joad story. It's true. Listen to Woody Guthrie singing "Tom Joad." It's beautiful and tells a story. Billy Joe has a lot of Woody Guthrie in him. He has the good and bad traits. The bad traits are never being able to get out of his own way. You'll tell him this guy has seven hundred million dollars, and he owns all these radio stations. He loves you and wants you to have your own show. Just let him take you out to lunch and behave decently. Billy Joe will wind up throwing the table up and pissing off the one guy he doesn't need to piss off. This lady wanted him on this series of television shows and [said] he was going to be a superstar. All he had to do was have lunch with her and be nice. He couldn't do it. She wanted him to wear overalls, and he reacted violently. He really upset her, and she said, "Forget that guy." I don't know why he does that, but Woody did the same.

I am depressed about modern-day Nashville. I try not to go there, but, when I do, [I see] cranes blotting out the sky. I'm currently writing a song about it. Not that anybody gives a shit about Nashville, or about anybody writing a song, because songs have become much less important. That's what we've learned from what's coming out of Nashville. [They're] not real songs. Yes, these guys are unbelievable. They sell millions of records, but the pendulum is swinging back to more independent thinking and really good writers like Roger Miller, Shel Silverstein, and Billy Joe.

Fortunately, Billy and I came up in Nashville around the same time Kris Kristofferson was the most talented janitor in [town]. Songwriting was carefully guarded. There's a story about Willie and Merle [Haggard] walking down the street when Kristofferson exploded. Everybody was raving about him, and Merle was depressed. He told Willie, "I guess Kris really is the greatest songwriter in town." Willie says, "After you and me." The last time I saw Billy Joe and Willie together, Billy Joe was driving home just smashed out of his mind. Willie was trying to get him to smoke some more dope with him. I told him, "Don't do it, Billy Joe. Just go home and get some fucking rest." Billy Joe passed on the dope, and Willie said, "Coward." Billy Joe left in a snit.

Billy Joe is a poet disguised as a country songwriter. There will not be a throwaway word in a Billy Joe Shaver song, but songwriters write differently now. They have a goal. There's this television show, and we need background music playing for this. There's a commercial, and we want to have a little country music. They try to appeal to a different segment. "We want to know what a young girl feels going to her first tailgating party." That's what the talent is, writing a fucking piece of shit that's already got a place for a lot of money if you can accurately describe what a fourteen-year-old girl is thinking. Musically speaking, Billy Joe can't play guitar. God took that away from him [losing his fingers], but the young kids in Texas and other places can. So you've got a kid who can play like Stevie Ray Vaughn in just about every town, and a girl who can sing like Janis Joplin. Buffalo probably has them. If you want to call that talent, okay, but it's karaoke talent that doesn't inspire. Maybe you've got to be a certain age to inspire. You go see Billy Joe, and you come out a slightly different person, like you saw a great film. You come out thinking you're there.

Our culture is changing. I don't know that there's a place for a poet in music. As Captain Midnight said of Tom T. Hall, "I love all of his songs and both of his melodies." Today you can't even tell that joke, because people don't know who he is. Australia is getting like that, but when we were playing there, people traveled hundreds of miles to see Billy Joe. They're not coming to watch a kid with a guitar that's hot, they're coming to watch a farm boy who's written poetry they relate to. He's as popular as anybody who's gone through there. They love his songs. His songs are smart, and he's beatific like a god. He's a saint. Like Robert Lewis Stevenson [is supposed to have] said, "Saints are sinners who kept on going."

Billy Joe is as close to Jesus as anybody's going to get and manages to do the Christian stuff without being preachy. Never any hint of it. Not like the gospel that so many people are doing. He presents Jesus in a completely humanistic light. He's written some beautiful stuff that appeals to me as a Jew. It's raw poetry, and it's amazing that as many songs as he's written get played. "I'm Just an Old Chunk of Coal (but I'm Gonna Be a Diamond Someday)" is just a hell of a song. He has hundreds like that. As my father Tom Friedman once said, "Never underestimate the power of gentile prayer." Billy Joe believes in and loves that quote. He's been steeped in this stuff since he was a little kid. Billy Joe was one of my father's favorites. When my dad was dying of cancer, Billy Joe came to the hospital and played some songs for him. It was very touching. He's a wonderful man, and there's nobody writing on his level.[3]

Kinky Friedman, born November 1, 1944, in Chicago, grew up on a ranch in Kerrville, Texas, and formed his first band, King Arthur and the Carrots, while attending University of Texas at Austin. By 1973, he had started his second band, Kinky Friedman and the Texas Jewboys, and he released his landmark debut album, Sold American, *that same year. During the eighties, Friedman took a departure from songwriting to pursue a career as a novelist and has since published more than twenty-five books in the mystery and detective genre. In 2003, Friedman and Shaver released the album* Live from Down Under *from their Australian tour. In 2006, Friedman ran for governor of Texas, with Shaver serving as his campaign's spiritual advisor. His last album,* Circus of Life (2018), *produced by singer-songwriter Brian Molnar, was his first collection of all new material in nearly four decades. He is the subject of Mary Lou Sullivan's 2017 biography* Everything's Bigger in Texas: The Life and Times of Kinky Friedman.*

Whey Jennings

I've known Billy Joe Shaver my entire life and grew up with his music. My parents were married at a very young age and divorced when I was three years old. My mom got custody of me. I'd see my dad [Waylon Jennings's son Terry] every other week. I lived a normal life in a lower-income neighborhood, went to school, played football, and got in trouble. I'd see my grandfather in airports, hotels, and backstage. I witnessed his life from behind the scenes. I saw both sides.

Billy Joe is a cocky Texan just like the rest of us. He's adamant about what he does, is strong about his songs, and was built for the outlaw movement. He stirred the pot and got all the real people to come out.

Whey Jennings.
Photo by Mickey
Webb.

He had balls. When I was young, my grandfather heard one of his songs and liked it. He told Billy to come to Nashville. Billy said, "Yeah, tomorrow." Billy Joe came to Nashville looking for my grandfather. He finally tracked him down in a studio. Billy Joe was aggravated because it took him so long to find him. My grandfather was protected by bikers. Billy Joe walked through all those bikers, and said, "Waylon, you're gonna listen to my songs, or I'm gonna whup your ass." With no record deal, he got my grandfather to cut an album of all his songs but one. He stood up to my grandfather, and [Waylon] loved him for it. I love "Honky Tonk Heroes." Rather than just playing it straight through, my grandfather took it in stages. Second round, third round, and the song got more and more intense. They had a disagreement about it, but I think he knocked it out of the park.

If Billy Joe believed in something and wanted it done, he got it done. Everyone in the outlaw movement stood up for what they believed in. Today as outlaw country artists we're still fighting for the freedom to be ourselves, but there are so many different fights in so many different areas. Back then, there was one person herding the cattle. Today there's a lot of people herding a lot of cattle, but Billy Joe and Willie Nelson are living proof that you don't have to change. They're the epitome of country music. They knew what they wanted and did it. They're still doing it to this day. Money doesn't matter. They are who they are. They're not trying to be anybody else. They called it a movement, but it wasn't planned. It was a bunch of artists who stood for the same morals and standards. They were themselves and give us younger artists the will to do it. You can look at somebody who was put through the wringer and beat the hell out of themselves and come out inspired.

Billy Joe's nice to everybody unless they're not nice to him. I've always liked that about him. No matter what situation that you're in, he's the same. He put it out there for the world to see, which is a beautiful thing. It takes gumption to say, "Look at all my ugly." Most people lock that up in the closet and burn it [before] they die. Billy Joe is a real man. He showed me it was possible to put [your beliefs] in your music. Growing up, even the mention of God or Jesus shut everybody's ears off. Nobody wants to hear it. I have my own connections with God. He spills over into my songs. If you ask anyone after drinking a beer, there's two things they won't talk about—religion and politics—but these are necessary things. There's going to come a point in everybody's life where they question what they've done and blame the Bible. Billy Joe got to that point and spilled it all out onstage. Everything that came into his mind came out in his songs. That's why people respect him so much. He never went out there and tried to put on a show that wasn't him. He never [went] out there and put on a pink shirt and acted like a different person. He writes in universal language and brings stories to people, so they can hear what they've never seen.

Songwriters have to sacrifice. If somebody never experienced anything, they're not going to be able to write a song. You have to go out there and get your ass whooped before you can write. If you're trying to be something you're not, you're going hear it. Music is everything to me. I live my life by my songs. When I'm in a situation and see something that stands out, I write about it. Everything I write is real. That's what Billy Joe did—whatever he was feeling right then. He's still out there just like I am, with his nose to the grindstone, going from bar to bar, show to show. I think he's probably gonna fall over onstage one day. Hopefully that won't be for twenty or thirty years, but I guarantee he ain't ever gonna stop, because he loves the feeling he gets when people enjoy what he does. When you've done a lot of wrong in life, you can see people enjoying something you're doing right. You never want to stop doing it. Billy Joe has done everything wrong in life, and everything right in his music. He's sinned enough to be doomed to suffer in his own mind and heart. The world would be at a loss if he was never alive because nobody would have heard the pain that he felt through his career. He lost his son and wife. He lost everything, but he never lost his music. He's never going to.[4]

Whey Jennings, the grandson of Waylon Jennings and Jessi Colter, maintains a deep love for music. When he was a boy at one of his grandfather's shows, he picked up a microphone left on a chair by Colter and walked onstage singing Waylon's hit, "Mammas Don't Let Your Babies Grow Up to Be Cowboys." He was joined by his grandfather, to the crowd's applause, and fell in love with music that day. Rough around the edges and with unpolished grit, Jennings plays authentic southern rock rooted in traditional country and carries on the unapologetic outlaw tradition his grandparents were known for.

Ted Russell Kamp

I first met Billy Joe playing bass for Shooter Jennings. Every time I see him, he asks me about Jessi Colter with excitement. "How is ole Jessi?" I love that about him. I fell in love with his songwriting through Waylon's version of "Black Rose." Here's this guy who's in trouble, tempted by a woman, and singing about the "darker side of shame." You don't know their relationship. He took risks with country-specific imagery that's left open. Waylon had a gift singing Billy Joe's song, but Billy Joe had a gift for speaking in deceptively powerful slang. He has a richness of language and emotional intensity a lot of guys don't. I graduated from college with an English and philosophy degree. Billy Joe could go that way. He could slow it down like Guy Clark or Kris Kristofferson, but he chooses not to.

He doesn't get too complicated and does his own thing. His songs have moments that bring you in with emotional heaviness, and then he'll follow it with something fun and charming, or something so fast you don't realize it's serious, but it has depth. The looseness of "I Been to Georgia on a Fast Train" invites you on a fun ride. It's a party, but

Ted Russell Kamp at the California Country Showcase during AmericanaFest, Nashville, Tennessee, September 2017. Photo by Mark Whitfield Lennon.

there's something serious going on. These are the reasons he's so loved, appreciated, emulated, and covered.

Kris gets down and dirty, but he's a bohemian. You feel him being of the hippie generation with the way he talks. Billy Joe can write details about poverty that aren't just convincing, they're intoxicating. You want to learn more about that life. The way he talks is so real. It's like seeing a Mafia movie. You don't know how people live in that world, but you're drawn to it because it's so different. When he gets to the punch line, he doesn't just make it an image, he makes it an impactful moment.

A lot of country music is straight rhythmically, which leaves room for a lot of heart and honesty. That's the beauty of bluegrass. It's not soul music, but there's a ton of heart in it. Waylon, along with his drummer Richie Albright and some of the bass players who played on his classic records, were on their own inventing a new approach to country music. I've never had this validated, but one of my big theories is that they listened to things that weren't country, like The Band, Joe Cocker, and Leon Russell. I know that Waylon was a big fan of J. J. Cale and that Willie Nelson did a couple records with Leon Russell. It was the very early seventies, and Waylon was absorbing that thing where the drummer plays a funky half-time beat while the bass player is still playing in 2/4 time. You don't hear it like that with Billy's versions. Billy Joe never really explored that musical territory, but they were musical templates that were so good, you could do them however you wanted, and the power shines through.

Waylon was inspired by the songs, and the band was having fun, but it was authentic storytelling. Some of the pitfalls in modern country writing, is that it's all fun and shit-kicking. "I'm fucked up at the bar, and here's another song." It's been done really well by many artists, but Billy Joe had a way of combining those worlds. We're not just partying at the honky-tonk. There's always a reason why he's there and a confusion. He's battling with the darker and spiritual sides of his soul. There's a great mixture of dark and light that includes laughing at himself. You're not sure if it's the third person or the first person. Many singer-songwriters strive to do that and are not as successful as he is.

When I got to Nashville, I knew I wasn't really country. I couldn't write a song about the gravel roads on a Saturday night drinking Coors light with the girl in Daisy Dukes. That's something a lot of country songwriters grew up with. The only songs I have like that are collaborations where I wrote the melody. I was helping connect dots to make a better song, not coming up with the subject matter. If you take my inability to do the small-town country stuff out of songwriting, Billy Joe has influenced me. His humor and instinct for melody has rubbed off on me. He keeps his chords very simple. It's poignant and what I love about country music.

About four years ago, I got a call from Gary Nicholson asking me about a guitar player to go on a short run with Billy Joe. I recommended my friend John Scheffler. Billy Joe doesn't want a guitarist who is doing a lot when he's singing. When it's time to play lead, you do your Chuck Berry thing or you do your honky-tonk riffs. He doesn't take himself too seriously, doesn't do any diva crap, just shows up, plays the gig, loves it, smiles for pictures, goes to the next town, and does the same thing. There's something very in the moment with him. He rolls with it and loves it. He doesn't need a big expensive tour bus. He's still very country and earthy, which comes across in his songwriting.

Billy Joe's a survivor who's been through shit, but he can laugh at it and power through. He doesn't need a band. He's a natural storyteller talking about a time that's past. The time of growing up a sharecropper in honky-tonks is gone. Corb Lund is great. He's really country, but he grew up on a ranch in Alberta, Canada, with modern farming. It's a different kind of safety and cattle-raising. Back in the sixties, it was the Wild West. I ran into a guy at a festival whose uncle was Waylon's tour manager. He told me stories about bikers running clubs, and they didn't want to pay him. "Here's a gun. Go in there and make sure you get paid. I don't give a fuck what happens. We're going to get paid and get out alive." I've done a lot of gigs, and that's never happened in my life, but I feel that in Billy Joe's songs. There's a piece of history and a way of life that's changed. You can glamorize it in a writer like him, but he's not trying to glamorize it. He's honest.[5]

Ted Russell Kamp grew up in New York and studied philosophy and English at the State University of New York at Binghamton. Kamp moved to Los Angeles where he became a highly regarded sideman in addition to writing his own songs. Kamp is known for his precise and soulful bass playing, which he lends to Shooter Jennings's band. An acclaimed singer-songwriter in his own right, Kamp has released twelve studio albums, and his 2018 release, Walking Shoes, *showcases his southern-fried rock and soul sound inspired by J. J. Cale, Leon Russell, and The Band.*

Mark Chesnutt

Billy Joe Shaver is a renegade. He's totally different from anybody else. He was a free spirit, giving songs to people like Waylon that expressed their feelings and pissed off Nashville. The outlaw movement wasn't about commercial music. Billy Joe's not trying to write by appointment like they do in Nashville. They write five or six a day trying to make a hit record. He writes the way he wants to write. Sometimes it's out of meter, but every word has meaning. There's no filler. It all comes from the heart. His songs teach you what real music is supposed to sound like. He writes from the soul. It's raw and real.

I used to write all the time listening to Waylon's recordings of Billy Joe Shaver songs. I think Waylon did them better than anybody and kept the rawness. Everybody else polished it up too much. There's not a whole lot of instrumentation. It goes with the drifter's attitude and freedom

Mark Chesnutt. Photo by Jim McGuire.

of Billy's songs. What little writing style I have, I got from Billy Joe. I've always cowritten with people like Roger Springer. He's another guy who can write alone. Me and him would get together, and the ideas I came up with were in Billy Joe's style. Real simplistic with a basic rhythm.

I cut "Black Rose" on my album *Outlaw* from the Waylon version. I've always loved that song, and I recorded an acoustic version of "Honky Tonk Heroes" to close out [*Savin' the Honky Tonk*]. I made it sound old-fashioned and put the coolness on it. The album cover [intentionally looks like] the cover of *Honky Tonk Heroes*. I always thought it was cool because it wasn't posed. They were just hanging out. So I thought, *Let's do that*. A friend of mine had a bar in Nashville. I got my group together, with my producer, manager, and a photographer. The bar was closed. We needed to make [it] authentic, so they brought in bartenders who started pouring beers for everyone at ten in the morning. People were smoking, drinking, and getting wasted just to get pictures. It came out great. We had a blast.

I've been around Billy Joe a few times at the Grand Ole Opry. It was nice to meet and talk to him. I told him how much of a fan I was of his songs. He seemed surprised. He was friendly and polite, just a laid-back country boy who never tried to be a big star, but he's a legend and carries it off well. Nobody wrote songs like "Black Rose," "Honky Tonk Heroes" and "Ride Me Down Easy." Even though they were commercial, they weren't meant to be. God bless him. His songs will live forever.[6]

Mark Chesnutt, born September 6, 1963, in Beaumont, Texas, is known for his blend of traditional and pop country. In the nineties, Chesnutt charted eight number-one singles on the Billboard *Hot Country Songs chart, including "Brother Jukebox," "It's a Little Too Late," "Almost Goodbye," and "It Sure Is Monday." Chesnutt's 1992 album* Longnecks and Short Stories *went platinum and includes collaborations with George Jones ("Talkin' to Hank") and Alison Krauss with Vince Gill ("It's Not Over"). His 1994 album,* What a Way to Live, *saw Chesnutt collaborating with Waylon Jennings on a new version of the Jennings's classic "Rainy Day Woman." His most recent album* Tradition Lives *climbed to number twenty-two on the* Billboard *Top Country Albums chart.*

James Carothers

I first became aware of Billy Joe's songwriting from *Honky Tonk Heroes*. It's one of the greatest collections of songs ever. I went to my local record store and said, "Man, this guy is genius." Then this guy says, "You should listen to his singing. He's a great singer." At that time, he was playing with Eddy. That interested me because my dad was a songwriter too. Not a famous one, but I played guitar for him. I loved Eddy's guitar playing, and Billy Joe's singing was phenomenal. I was hooked and got more of his records.

Billy Joe's music is a piece of the American West. It describes a whole generation of people who lived across America. It's historical and cultural because of the stories he tells and the context he tells them in. The lyrics are so authentic because he's a born Texas hillbilly and has a way of speaking and phrasing naturally. The way he uses his words is unique compared to other songwriters. He's been a huge influence because of

James Carothers. Photo by Josh Lackhart.

old-timey phrases [in song titles] like "Fit to Kill and Going Out in Style" and "I'm Just an Old Chunk of Coal." That stuff gives you the confidence and validation that you don't have to worry about your phrases being dated, because out in the country certain regions of people still use that language from 1930. It's classical old English like Shakespeare. Billy Joe's got the whole package, but what [really] separates him is his sense of melody. His melodies are far and away better than anybody else's. Some are swing, some are ragtime. You can whistle to all his songs. They're familiar.

"Honky Tonk Heroes" is the song I play the most. I sing it, and it feels like I could have written the song to people who don't know Waylon or Shaver. They think, *He's singing about himself.* It's a universal theme for people who work in honky-tonk bars playing music. That's how you feel going into the gig. You're drawn to these places like a moth, and you kind of get burned every time. People relate. They feel the same way. "No-account boozers and honky-tonk heroes" describes people from every walk of life and why they came in. It's woeful, but those lyrics at a faster pace with a good beat take them from sad to happy with three minutes of an amazing song. It's easy for me to imagine why Waylon would record it and name his best record after it.

I've never met Billy Joe, but my friend Kenny here in Nashville is an old wiry bull rider who became friends with him. I see Kenny, and he's got this 1955 Gibson J-45 guitar worth about $5,000. There was a bumper sticker on the case that said, "If you don't love Jesus go to Hell." I ask him, "Dude where'd you get that?" "Billy Joe gave it to me [at Knuckleheads Saloon in Kansas City, Missouri]." "No way." I'd been playing there for years and never saw Shaver. Kenny pulled up pictures on his phone. Shaver backed over the guitar with his car, took it to the guitar shop, and they fixed it up. Kenny's not famous, so there was no advantage for Billy Joe to give that guitar to him. He's just a nice fella and his heart went out to him. I couldn't believe it.[7]

James Carothers began his recording career at age thirty-three after leaving a job in New Mexico and moving back to his home state of Tennessee. Carothers is known for his outlaw country originals and voice that recalls country icons like George Jones. Carothers's 2018 album, Still Country, Still King, *is a tribute to Jones. His 2017 album,* Relapse, *features the modern-day outlaw country anthem "Back to Hank."*

I Been to Georgia on a Fast Train

J. P. Harris

Billy Joe Shaver changed my understanding of what songwriting could be. He broke the mold when people were still following rules about kickoffs and catchy choruses. He wrote what he wanted to and founded the Texas country sound. About a decade ago I realized I was singing along to all these tunes and thought, I wonder if Waylon really wrote all these songs? I looked it up and said, *Holy shit. Who is this Billy Joe Shaver?*

Fast-forward to when I finally discovered "I Been to Georgia on a Fast Train" through a late-in-life Tennessee Ernie Ford version. I got the record and saw Billy Joe Shaver's name. I thought, *You've got to be kidding me. Billy Joe Shaver? What did he* not *write?* I went home and found a recording on YouTube of Billy playing it in the early nineties. He's got these young dudes playing in his band, and Eddy's playing this crazy-ass solo with a dirty guitar tone. He turned this band of young Texas dudes totally wild and loose. He's up there owning the shit out of the stage with his guitar slung around his back. Eddy's just shredding it, but it's country, and it hit me, *This is Billy Joe Shaver.* I was a fan right there.

"I Been to Georgia on a Fast Train" connects me with Billy Joe Shaver, and it will for the rest of my life. It's badass, the kind of song you want to bring into a dancehall, and the words are close to my life. I finished the eighth grade, left home at fourteen, rode freight trains all over the country, and herded sheep for old Navajo ladies. I did all kinds of wild shit. I lived in the woods for eleven years with no running water

J. P. Harris (*at microphone*) performing with his band the Tough Choices, OMEARA, London, November 16, 2018. Photo by Raghad Tmumen.

or electricity before coming to Nashville to be closer to my family in Alabama. So when I heard it, I said, *This is my Billy Joe Shaver anthem.* Many times, I'm in the middle of a long death march tour, get up, cue that tune, crank it all the way to eleven, and jam it to get the day started. It's always a good shot in the arm. Billy Joe's a badass wild man. The real deal. His life was a lot crazier than mine, but when I hear it, I think, *I bet me and Billy Joe would have a lot of interesting things to talk about—where we've been, and what we've done.*

Billy Joe has the ability to translate every aspect of his own life into layman's terms for the people around him and turn it into poetry. That's the ultimate accomplishment in country songwriting. It's not just catchy hooks or clever turns of phrase, it's turning your own tales into something digestible for the everyman. I love all the talented singers of yesteryear, but I've always been drawn to people with quirky individual voices. People who didn't sing what's conventional or technically advanced. They didn't cop the tricks from George Jones and Ray Price. Billy Joe never tried to mold his voice into something it wasn't. He just sang as Billy Joe Shaver. That stood out from the first time I heard him.

Picking a favorite Shaver tune is apples and oranges. There are at least twenty-one greatest. "Honky Tonk Heroes" is a hilarious, badass tune. There wasn't a lot of humor in the early days of country music. The early country music I first got into wasn't goofy. You look back and realize some of them are, but they weren't intended to be. I heard "Honky Tonk Heroes," and it was one of the first times I connected with a song that wasn't necessarily a well-put-together composition like an old Ray Price tune. He opened up my mind to a different songwriting approach.

One of the first songs I wrote, "Badly Bent" [from the Harris album *I'll Keep Calling*], turned out to be a hit single. It got more airplay than anything else I've ever recorded and has become the anthem for my fans. Everybody loves it. It's a smart-ass tune about day-to-day life. The chorus is "These clothes ain't dirty, honey, they're just stained from the honky-tonk lifestyle that I maintain." I wrote it not long after I heard Waylon's "Honky Tonk Heroes." It shifted a gear [for] me, that I could be a little bit more autobiographical and put my tongue [in] my cheek when I wrote tunes. I didn't have to write classic songs about heartbreak. They didn't need to follow a format. I could individually tell my tale. I'm a smart-ass and tell dirty jokes from stage. That's who I am, and that tune taught me I could show the world who I was. I was hearing it by Waylon and thinking I was influenced by him. I hadn't realized at that point that I was actually being influenced by Billy Joe Shaver, but I was. So, very early on, my songwriting was expanded by his cleverness. It was the first time a song like that stuck to me. I owe Billy Joe.

It's important Billy Joe's songs are preserved, because the last of the real-deal country songwriters are dying out. The world of what we identify now as country singers is watered down by people who share a thin common thread with the old-timers. Today's country singers are so much more conventional and grew up in incredibly normal environments, no heavy-duty backwoods hardship in life. Their commonality with old-timers is that they like fried okra and drove a pickup truck. The reason the country singers of yesterday became who they became and shaped the music into what it was is because they had a connection to what came before them, and [this] eventually got amalgamated, reshaped, and shaved down into classic country, old-time barn-dance music, and western swing.

Nowadays there's a disconnect. You might see some Luke Bryan son-of-a-bitch in a Waylon T-shirt, but they aren't really influenced by [Waylon]. They like to tout that they grew up on country music, but knowing what it is, absorbing the tradition, and making it your own are two different things. I can count on one hand country songwriters of my generation that will be the real-deal country dudes, but the way the world is structured now, none of us will be as well-received or recognized as Willie and Waylon. The world won't allow us to be those people in history. There's such a small group of us who lived lives that country music became the soundtrack of and understand people like Billy Joe Shaver. A lot of the old-time country greats lived normal lives too, but Billy Joe and Waylon grew up to be country singers. They're part of the American landscape. Old-school country to twentysomethings today is John Anderson or Brooks and Dunn. I listen to it, but I'm not influenced by it. I went further back. It bridged the disconnect.

You had music that felt country and authentic. Then, in the last thirty years, it got watered down and turned into garbage. It's just bad music. These dudes are making millions of dollars, so it's not bad to some people, but country music has the power to span class, background, and political orientation more than any other type of music in America. It's music for working folk. Outside of the racial lines that still exist, it brings people from different ends of society to a middle ground where everyone can sing along, drink a cold one, and two-step. In the bigger picture, it makes the world harmonious. I don't believe this tractor rap bullshit is doing anything to bring anyone together. It's giving people an excuse to be dumber and think less. Billy Joe Shaver is a hillbilly, but he ain't dumb. He's a highly intelligent hillbilly. It's a fine balance. That's what makes his songs identifiable to so many.

Maybe twenty years from now some kid will come up behind me and read a book about Billy Joe, and suddenly they'll find that spark of inspiration. They'll hear stories from other people Billy Joe knew, and it will open their mind. It might give them food for thought, to reach beyond what they've been fed and go deeper. This is old country music. There are people who are ahead of their time yet still timeless. Billy Joe is at the top of that list.[1]

J. P. Harris, born on February 13, 1983, in Montgomery, Alabama, left home right after finishing eighth grade, traveling the country by hitchhiking and hopping freight trains while making a living doing odd jobs and manual labor. In 2012, he released his debut album I'll Keep Calling, *and then the 2014 follow-up* Home Is Where the Hurt Is, *saw him rise to stardom and earned him the praise of critics and fans alike. After a four-year break, in 2018 he released* Sometimes Dogs Bark at Nothing, *produced by Morgan Jahnig of Old Crow Medicine Show. The album is a mix of traditional country and 1960s folk, opening up with "JP's Florida Blues #1," a hard-driving country rock song that details his darker days touring Florida with his band the Tough Choices.*

Matt Minglewood

Old Five and Dimers Like Me is the first Billy Joe Shaver record I heard. It was just amazing that he could put his words together like he does. I heard "I Been to Georgia on a Fast Train" and ended up recording it. I was already going to do a rock and country record of my own songs, and it just fit. I put it out as a single up here in Canada [in 1986], and it did quite well [reaching number twenty-four on the Canada Country chart]. It set the tone for the way I wanted the record to be. You can hear Billy Joe songs sung by somebody else, and even though they are a great singer it just comes across as so original and real when you hear Billy Joe sing it.

I did a show with Billy Joe up in Saskatchewan, Canada, back in 1986 on a reservation. There were other reservations around, and people came up for this big bash. Some of the other reservations that came didn't like each other. It got weird. The night was supposed to be all-ages, but there was liquor, and people were really drunk. They weren't very respectful, even though Billy Joe is [part] Native American. His performance was incredible. I hung on every word. I don't know who was disrespecting him, but it broke my heart. The chief of the tribe didn't call off the show on the second night, but he called off the liquor.

The night was beautiful. I went up to Billy Joe, and he reached out his hand with the missing fingers. He said, "Sorry, I've been shortchanged." I said, "You haven't been shortchanged anything." I asked him if I could sing "I Been to Georgia on a Fast Train." He said, "By all means. I'd love

Matt Minglewood, promotional photo.

to hear it." He had his son Eddy playing with him. It was gorgeous. He's a real Texas songwriter. Whenever I hear a Billy Joe song come on, I'm going to listen. If it's a new song, I'm really going to listen to it because he'll never let you down. I have so much respect for him and Guy Clark. All of those great songwriters that never got their dues. Such wordsmiths. In one hundred years from now, I won't be here, but his songs will be. They are going to be [remembered] like [those of] Bob Dylan. People will listen, [learn] what it was like back then, and say, "Here's some real music folks. Real songs. They stand the test of time." I admire him. I wish I could write like him.[2]

Matt Minglewood, born January 31, 1947, in Moncton, New Brunswick, later relocated to Nova Scotia, where he currently resides. In his late teens,

Minglewood joined his first band, the Rockin' Saints. When he was in his early twenties, he was part of a band called Sam Moon, Matt Minglewood & the Universal Power. The group was formed in 1969, with Sam Moon and Minglewood sharing vocal duties. The band soon changed their name to Moon-Minglewood and becoming a staple at local high school dances. In 1974 he formed the Minglewood Band and toured Canada extensively. The Minglewood Band recorded their first album with Solar Records in 1975 and soon signed with RCA Records. He has released twelve albums over his career, has had five singles land in the top fifty on the Canada Country chart, and has been nominated for numerous Canadian Country Music Association and Juno Awards.

Vincent Neil Emerson

I've been singing "I Been to Georgia on a Fast Train" since I was nineteen. I relate to that lyrically because of what I've been through in my life. I dropped out of high school in tenth grade, and my mom wasn't exactly around a whole lot when I was growing up. I think for the most part Billy Joe's music is autobiographical, but, [as] singer-songwriters, we reserve the right to use our imaginations and come up with things.

I met Billy Joe doing a show with Eleven Hundred Springs at Granada in Dallas. It was my third time playing there and first time playing with Billy Joe. We squeaked on the bill. I assumed that he would be a tough person to talk to, but I walked up to him, and he shook my hand. "Hey, how you doing, boy?" We got to talking about old honky-tonk [music] and hung out for hours. By the end of the night, he had his arm wrapped around my neck, telling me he loved the show. I met a few Texas legends, and he's by far the nicest and most supportive. You don't see that a lot. With how influential he is, it's amazing how nice he was. It blew my mind. Hopefully, if I ever get to where Billy Joe is as far as the amount of respect that we have for him, I can be like him in that way. [Be] that humble, and still be a person who talks with people. I wrote a song called "Highway Shine" [from the Emerson album *Fried Chicken and Evil Women*]. It has the line, "Coming back from Amarillo, I just talked to Billy Joe, he told me to listen to this song that he wrote, 'I'm Just an Old Chunk of Coal.'"

Vincent Neil Emerson and Jesse Daniel poster. Photo by Courtney S. Lennon.

"I'm Just an Old Chunk of Coal (but I'm Gonna Be a Diamond Someday)" is probably one of my favorite tunes of his. Before I even really started listening to the words, I just liked the rhythm and chord changes. It caught me, and the lyrics mean a lot to me. [It's about] wanting to be a better person, changing yourself, trying to change for the better.

It's something that I think about fairly often. I think everybody does sometimes. It just makes sense.

I'm from East Texas, and there's a bond between Texas songwriters. I've always been a big fan of Townes Van Zandt, Guy Clark, and the folksinger-songwriters. Billy Joe fits right in. He's a good ole boy playing honky you can dance to, but he's just as much of a singer-songwriter as Townes and Guy. He comes up with amazing lyrics. I'm not sure he knows how special they are sometimes. Billy Joe has a knack for story-telling. Some people can overdo it, like Ramblin' Jack Elliott. He'll sit there, sing two songs the whole night, and just talk. Billy Joe weaves that in between the songs very well. It's incredible. It's a shame more people aren't aware of his significance. He changed the face of country music by marrying honky-tonk and rock and roll. It gave it a driving rhythm. I believe that wholeheartedly. Waylon really took off with *Honky Tonk Heroes*. If we didn't have Waylon doing all of that, where would we be? We probably wouldn't have guys like Cody Jinks, Whitey Morgan, or Shooter Jennings. We wouldn't have those dudes. People can attribute that to Waylon himself, but I like to look at the source.

I'm inspired by Billy Joe's no-nonsense writing. That's what I emulate. I love Willie Nelson to death. Willie gets all the credit he deserves, but I think Billy Joe should be right next to [him]. At the end of the day, Billy wrote the songs that he wanted to write, and did the things that he wanted to do. He didn't miss anything.[3]

Vincent Neil Emerson, born April 30, 1992, is a Fort Worth–based country singer-songwriter who came to notoriety when Aquaman *actor Jason Momoa featured him in a video alongside friend and fellow singer-songwriter Colter Wall. In 2019, he released his debut album* Fried Chicken and Evil Women *on La Honda Records.*

Robert Ellis

Billy Joe Shaver is an anomaly. He has a gift for elevating the mundane to ethereal. "Live Forever" has the turn of phrase "When this old world is blown asunder" that on one hand sounds very southern, like your grandfather might say it, but it's also insanely poetic. He can fly under

Robert Ellis. Photo by Erica Silverman.

the radar and appeal to your most redneck friends and appeal to your most liberal elite friends because of his depth. Whatever you're listening for, you can find and enjoy on the surface. He wrote "Warrior Man," the theme song for the show *Squidbillies*. There's a line in there where he says, "I wish the sun would just explode." It's such a beautiful descriptive way to say how you feel. It says so much about him and his frustration. He's looking at this thing that's a beautiful source of life in the world and wishing it would explode. It's so telling. I think I've written things in songs and then said, "Oh, that's pretty much the same line. I need to change that. I can't just directly take that."

You can listen to "I Been to Georgia on a Fast Train" and think it's a wonderful country song, but you can also look at the lyrics and see that it's profound. The idea of "a good Christian raisin' and an eighth-grade education, ain't no need in y'all a-treatin' me this way" is funny, and a complex idea. He's indignant about having this redneck upbringing. I grew up in Clute, Texas, a very rural, small, and conservative town south of Houston. It's almost like he's risen above it. If you grow up in a really, small Texas town, and you read amazing books from a writer from New York, you can appreciate it. You can love it, but sometimes it's difficult to see yourself in them. Billy Joe gives me the feeling that there's somebody like me in the world. It's somebody from the same place as you, who is so wildly individual, unique, and accepted. It makes you feel less alone.

He creates art that tests and pushes us, but he's always been underappreciated. These other artists have huge followings and cult respect, and Billy Joe's always been an outsider, even in the outlaw country movement. He always had a left-of-center viewpoint that makes his songs so unique. They're just him, and I completely understand and relate to how hard it is to fit in when you have such a unique voice. I don't see many songwriters today who are as doggedly determined to be themselves as he was. As time moves on, and the more people are influenced by music, sometimes it's easy to forget how unique artists were over the course of one hundred years because of influence. All of a sudden, it's standard or traditional, but in their time, these people were really wing nuts. They were outsiders. Context is important.

Billy Joe subconsciously influenced me with his confidence, how wild and cocky he is. He dances and flails his arms with an imposing presence like public speaking. He pushes the meaning of the words. He's able to say them with meter and pacing that allows you to hear them. It's one thing to write something on a page, but to deliver it and get the meaning across is a different thing. He's great at both.

I played a show with Billy Joe years back at the Kessler Theater in Dallas. I was watching and thinking, *Holy shit. I know every one of these songs.* I made the connection about how prolific he is. Now when I hear other artists do his songs, they don't have the same poetry. When he sings "Live Forever," he flaps his wings like a bird. It's powerful. When I met him that night, he was insanely nice to me. He watched me play from side stage for at least a handful of my songs, and I was completely dumbfounded. After the show, he came up to me and shook my hand. Before I did the show, I'd had a few friends who knew him say, "Get ready," because I had heard some crazy stories about his interactions with people. Maybe I caught him on a good day, because I talked to him for a long time after, and he was really pleasant. That night, we were staying at the same boutique hotel, which was quite lovely. Billy Joe showed up with his [band] and crew in tow, walked in the door, and turned around. The place was too fancy for him. He went down the road and stayed at a La Quinta.[4]

Robert Ellis, born November 6, 1988, in Lake Jackson, Texas, is a Houston-based singer-songwriter who plays a mix of country, pop, and jazz. Ellis began performing under the moniker Eyes Like Lions in 2005 and self-released his debut, The Great Rearranger, *in 2009. His second album,* Photographs *(2011), was named one of the year's top fifty by* American Songwriter *magazine. In 2014, Ellis signed to New West Records and released* The Lights from the Chemical Plant, *an album inspired by his life growing up in Lake Jackson. In 2019, Ellis traded in his six-string guitar for a piano with his fifth studio album,* Texas Piano Man.

Mando Saenz

I first became familiar with Billy Joe Shaver's music in the mid-nineties when I was in college and *Tramp on Your Street* was out. CMT [had] just started a TV channel and used to play really good music. They don't seem to anymore. I saw the video for "I Been to Georgia on a Fast Train." The song and video were produced by R. S. Field, who produced *Freedom's Child*. I didn't know that until later, but it made sense, because the songs work so well with the graininess. I love the production on that album. It was a great marriage. I worked with R. S. on my *Bucket* record. He told me that Billy Joe asked everyone to bring a gun into the studio. Not sure the reason.

When I started writing songs, it became obvious what a great song-writer Billy Joe was and how much he'd done to up to that point. His songs are brilliant. They're simple in a genius way, which goes with his personality. His songwriting taught me that if you feel something, flesh it out, and write it down. A lot of times we have ideas, and we'll just put

Mando Saenz, promotional photo. Courtesy of Mando Saenz.

them away for later, but I think when you feel something strike you, you should power through and get it down while it's fresh in your head. Just sit down and write the thing. I did that with my song "Julia." I just wrote the words that came to my mind, and worried about it making sense after the fact. I like songs like that. He can [write] songs that don't seem like he spent eight hours in a coffee shop coming up with them. It strikes me. Even though everybody knows who he is, he doesn't get mentioned nearly as much as other people. He's one of the most under-rated songwriters in the outlaw movement.

I played a benefit in Houston with Billy Joe put on by the independent radio station KPFT. I was lucky enough to get the opening slot and played way too loud. I thought it would be a good idea. I was younger, I didn't know if it was tasteful or not. I was struck by how simple his set was. Power without blowing the doors. It was all about the songs and his voice. I learned a lot. I went up to him after. I said it was an honor to open for him. He couldn't have been sweeter.[5]

Mando Saenz, is a Nashville-based singer-songwriter who has released three albums, Watertown *(2005),* Bucket *(2008), and* Studebaker *(2013). Saenz writes for Carnival Music and has had songs recorded by Eli Young Band,*

Whiskey Myers, Wade Bowen, Lee Ann Womack, and Shelly Colvin. Saenz cowrote every track save one on Stoney LaRue's 2011 album Velvet, *which produced three number-one singles on the Texas Country Music Chart. His take on "Home Again" proved a high point on* Highway Prayer: A Tribute to Adam Carroll (*Eight 30 Records, 2016*).

Cecil Allen Moore

I first heard of Billy Shaver in the early nineties from my buddy Chris Green. We both grew up in Georgia, and he turned me on to "I Been to Georgia on a Fast Train." I later recorded it on my album *American Outlaw*. After I delved into his catalog, I realized what a huge impact he had on the music I grew up with. I was drawn in by the honesty of the lyrics, the purity of the songs, and the reality of his voice, which is undeniably real. He wasn't trying to sound like anyone but Billy Joe Shaver. When I write, I always make sure I'm being as true to myself as he's been. He knows exactly what to say and how to [tell] a story. You would have to be deaf not to learn something from him. His honesty, integrity, grit, knowledge, and experience guide me. Most writers try to build up to the bombshell they're trying to drop. He doesn't care to lay it all out there in the first little bit of the song. He has so much to say worth listening to and lays it on you. I've also learned simplicity, straightforwardness, and not caring to pronounce words exactly the way you say them in conversation from his writing. He's right up there with the great songwriters like Townes, Guy, John Prine, and Steve Young. I know plenty of folks will know that, but I hope that more people will also remember him for the fiery performances he puts on. I've done about a dozen or so shows with Billy Joe over the years and seen his show a dozen more times. It's something to behold.

The first time I met Billy Joe was in 1998. I was playing a coffeehouse in Chattanooga, Tennessee. Billy Joe was playing down the street at the next coffeehouse. Back then nobody enjoyed the outlaw country revival we have these days, so we played where we could. After my set, I walked down the block and popped in. He has a tremendous stage presence and knows how to make everyone in the room feel like he's talking and singing to them. By the end of the night, you can't help but feel a personal connection to him. I went and said howdy, and he became

Left to right: Cecil Allen Moore with Billy Joe Shaver, Riley's Tavern, New Braunfels, Texas, 2017. Photo courtesy of Cecil Allen Moore.

an instant buddy. He took time to talk and sign autographs for all who wanted [one]. I was greatly impressed with how humble, accessible, and gracious this legendary figure was. I told myself that if this guy who had written virtually every song on one of the best albums of all time could be so cool, there was no excuse for anyone not to be that way.

On another occasion in Chattanooga, we did an outdoor city event. Hank [Williams] III was playing down the road. I asked Billy Joe if [he'd] like to cruise down and catch the show. I could get us in. He replied, "I've seen Hank Sr., and Hank Jr., but never seen Three." We went and had a great time. [Hank Sr. died when Billy Joe was thirteen]. It was cool to be able to take [him] to that show and bring his Hank experience full circle. There was another time at a dinner show [when] he was flirting with the waitress. He told her he was blind and hoped her nametag was

in Braille so he could read her name. He's a funny character. God bless
Billy Joe Shaver.[6]

*Cecil Allen Moore, grew up in Chattanooga, Tennessee, and set out on his
career as a singer-songwriter in 1998, traveling the country as a solo artist
and playing lead guitar for outlaw country artists Roger Alan Wade and
David Allan Coe. Moore has released three solo albums and two albums
with the Tennessee Rounders in addition to appearing on countless recordings by other artists. In 2017, nine of his original recordings appeared in the
country music film* Buckshot.

Everybody's Brother

John Carter Cash

Billy Joe Shaver is the Wild West, one of America's greatest poets, and the voice of a conscious mind. I always appreciated his music. His words are uniquely Texas, a picture of the twentieth century with roots in the tree of early American music. Billy Joe was a fixture around my parents' house when I was growing up, and he was always stopping by to see dad. Dad recorded "I'm Just an Old Chunk of Coal" and connected with it on a spiritual level. "I'm gonna be a diamond someday" [illustrates] the impact of the darkness. The struggle we go through that can purify and refine our [souls].

Billy and my father were outlaws bound together. They didn't go buy a cowboy hat and beat up their boots. They wore the scars of survivors, and each had their own brand of success. Not money. Not sales. Creative spirit. I got closer to Billy when my sister Rosanne was dating Eddy Shaver. Later on, Billy Joe came to me with a passion to record a gospel album. Producing *Everybody's Brother* was the right fit. Billy Joe put his heart into it, and the album [earned him his first Grammy nomination]. He was honored and excited. Working with Billy Joe in the studio is like working with my father. He has emotional, intense energy that drives, pushes, and makes it happen. [Because] beneath that tough exterior, [his] heart's full of love and kindness that rules it all.

Billy Joe feels every word of the songs he writes. He has a gruff, rough voice, and a unique style that needs to be heard. He connects with you

John Carter Cash in recording studio, Nashville, Tennessee. Photo by David McClister.

when he sings, and that spirit dictated the music through the [recording] process, a free-moving, organic, creative endeavor. I don't mold artists. I perceive their particular vision and clarify it. Billy Joe's glasses helped us make the decisions we made [with] how the songs and band were chosen. I wanted it to be about him. Not the surrounding music, with a rootsy feel and [sparseness] as a picture to accompany the songs. It put Billy Joe up front.

My dad had passed, [but he and Billy Joe recorded "You Just Can't Beat Jesus Christ" in 1980], and that song is on the album. We brought a lot of friends into the studio to record, Kris Kristofferson ["No Earthly Good"], Tanya Tucker ["Played The Game Too Long"], and Marty Stuart ["Winning Again"]. I'd known John Anderson ["Get Thee behind Me, Satan" and "Jesus Is the Only One That Loves Us"] since I was ten years old. We used to hunt together when I was a boy. All of the artists on the album had love and kinship, living and breathing creativity.

Recording "Everybody's Brother" was the first time I met Bill Miller, [who] was the best man at my wedding. The passion between Bill and Billy Joe that that day is unforgettable. It's one of my favorite creative experiences. Billy Joe has a tough exterior and isn't perfect. He doesn't attest to be. Christ's blood is everybody's brother, and in his heart Billy Joe is everybody's brother.[1]

John Carter Cash, born March 3, 1970, in Nashville, is the son of Johnny Cash and June Carter Cash. Cash began his career as a producer with June Carter's 1999 Grammy-winning album Press On. *He went on to work with Rick Rubin on his father's Grammy-winning records* American III: Solitary Man *and* American IV: The Man Comes Around, *which won three Country Music Association awards. Cash produced Billy Joe Shaver's 2007 spiritual album* Everybody's Brother, *earning Shaver his first ever Grammy nomination.*

Marty Stuart

I first met Billy Joe when I joined Johnny Cash's band in 1980. His wife Brenda worked at the House of Cash in the publishing world, and Billy Joe wrote songs for Johnny Cash. He was beyond the ordinary cat, trying to find his place in this big universe. He could have been a preacher, a prize fighter, an outlaw, a songwriter, or a troubadour. He's all those things, and always felt bigger than the room. He fit right in with Johnny Cash.

I was at the first recording session that his son Eddy did. Billy Joe was like a nervous daddy watching his kid play on a Cash song. I felt the depth of his heart in his presence. Billy Joe's a profound pool of wisdom and a chief scribe of the outlaw movement. He wrote the script with flavor, movement, soul, and punch that all trace back to his heart. He's just a big walking heart. He's from the songwriting school of Woody Guthrie. Pete Seeger said Woody was a traveling boxcar correspondent reporting on the human condition. Billy Joe reports in black and white without an ounce of hype. We both try to tell the truth from a reporter's perspective, but Billy Joe stands alone. On my best day, on my best song, I would hope to come within a mile of him.

I remember when Billy Joe and I were up at Cowboy Jack Clement's recording studio, with no window between the control room and recording floor. Billy Joe brought his road band, and there was no way to see. We were listening to the session, and one of the musicians couldn't get it right. Billy Joe was very patient, loving, and tried to get him in line.

Marty Stuart. Photo by David McClister.

He said, "Wait a minute." The tape stopped, and Billy Joe went in. You could hear everything on the microphone. He thumped him on the head real good and said, "Now straighten up and get this right." I thought, *That's pretty good.*

Country music, folk, and rock and roll all collide at the roots level. When I first came to Nashville, everyone was encouraged to bring their culture to the table. That's why you had Bill Monroe and bluegrass music in Kentucky, Bob Wills from Texas, Johnny Cash from Arkansas, and Merle Haggard whose life story came with him wherever he went. Billy Joe represents a corner of life like Townes Van Zandt, Guy Clark, Steve Earle, and Rodney Crowell. With all the tragedy in his life, he somehow came [out] the other side, not wanting to jump off a bridge, encouraging other people to live on. He has a pure, "been there, done that" authentic wisdom in his songs, and they have a timeless ring to them. His unique slant on life and experiences gave him [obvious] gravity. When Billy Joe goes to the afterlife, and all the stories are told, generation after generation will find their mark behind him. His songs will live on and on.[2]

Marty Stuart, born September 30, 1958, in Philadelphia, Mississippi, is a multi-Grammy-winning singer-songwriter who began his career at age twelve playing mandolin in Lester Flatt's band, Nashville Grass. In 1980, Stuart joined Johnny Cash's band. Stuart's 1986 eponymous Columbia Records debut made it to number thirty-four on the Billboard *Country [Albums] chart, and his MCA Records follow-up,* Hillbilly Rock, *charted in the top twenty. He has since released eight more studio albums and performs on Shaver's 2007, John Carter Cash–produced spiritual album,* Everybody's Brother *(on "Winning Again").*

James McMurtry

Billy Joe Shaver knows how to phrase in his songs. His syllables fall right into the pocket. You can talk over and sing them, whatever you want. They're flexible, and the details jump out on the track. You can hear exactly what he's saying. His word dichotomy is the same as poets['], only it's songwriting, not poetry. Not many people can do that. Kristofferson, John Prine, and Billy Joe are great. Like Steve Earle said, "Most of us were doing what we were doing because of Bob Dylan, and we thought it was all right to do it in Nashville because of Kris Kristofferson. Billy Joe Shaver's unique in that he's a little older than Guy, but he'd never heard Bob Dylan. Somehow Billy Joe came out writing at this really high literary level anyway."[3]

Billy Joe's one of the realest people I've ever seen. My first image of him was in 1989 at Farm Aid at the old Hoosier Dome in Indianapolis.

Left to right: James McMurtry and Steve Earle, Sirius XM broadcast booth, Moody Theater, Austin, Texas, February 11, 2015. Photo by Brian T. Atkinson.

They talked me into doing Farm Aid. It was just some kind of ridiculous name, but I said I'd do it. I'm backstage, and there's this sea of spandex and weird hair. Everybody trying to pretend they give a damn about farmers or know anything about it. Through the middle of that crowd, I see Billy Joe. He looked thoroughly disgusted, and I said, "That guy might have actually done some farm work."

I had a confirmed and issued contract to play a show at the Love & War [in Texas] in Plano one time with Billy Joe Shaver and Ray Wylie Hubbard in 2005, but the venue owner insisted that I be thrown off that show due to my politics. My song "We Can't Make It Here" was viewed as an anti-Bush song. Usually you can sue people for that, but I don't have the money for litigation [or] the inclination. It eats up your life. It was probably a $1,500 gig, so I'd have to spend way more than that in legal fees, and I wasn't going to do that. I called Ray the next day and told him, "I want you to know I didn't quit this show, I got thrown off it." I was trying to get some solidarity going, but Ray hemmed and hawed. He was going to do the show anyway.

I didn't have Billy Joe's phone number, but it just so happened we were on the same label, Compadre Records, and they accidentally sent me Billy Joe's 1099 form, which gave me his address and phone number. I called him and left a message, "Hey, Billy, I just want you to know I didn't quit that show, I got thrown off of it because of my politics." The next morning, I had a message on my phone from Billy Joe. He said, "James I just want you to know I quit that show. That's bullshit." Billy's a stand-up guy.[4]

James McMurtry, born March 18, 1962, in Fort Worth, Texas, is a folk and Americana singer-songwriter and actor who appeared in the film Daisy Miller *and the television miniseries* Lonesome Dove, *the latter based on the novel by his father, Larry McMurtry. McMurtry spent the first seven years of his life in Texas, before moving to Leesburg, Virginia. McMurtry learned to play guitar from his mother, an English professor. In 1987, McMurtry won the Kerrville Folk Festival songwriting contest alongside five others, and in 1989 he released his debut album* Too Long in the Wasteland. *His 2002 album* St. Mary of the Woods *features his popular song "Choctaw Bingo." McMurtry's songs often follow political themes, and the song "We Can't Make It Here" is a criticism of former president George W. Bush and the Iraq War.*

Kimmie Rhodes

The first time I met Billy Joe I was working with Willie [Nelson]. We were cutting my song "I Just Drove By" that had gotten Willie's attention. Bucky [Meadows] came down to the studio for Billy Joe to play a song for me. Then Willie comes in and says to me, "Play another song for me." I did, and he said, "Well, let's just go in there and cut those right now" and swooped me off into the session. Billy Joe hears it, comes up to me, and gives me a backhanded compliment, "You know, just about the time I think I'm doing really well, some asshole like you comes along with a song like that."

Back in the mid-nineties, I was smoking pot all day with Billy Joe, Bucky, and my late husband Joe Gracey. Billy and Bucky [are] getting drunk on tequila, and I get this idea to make peach ice cream. They were going to churn it. So we're stoned, drunk, and sitting on the porch

Kimmie Rhodes. Photo by Jme Lacombe.

as it's getting dark. I've got them cranking the ice cream freezer. Then I realized I forgot to put in the ice cream. I see the mixture sitting there on the counter, go to the porch and say, "I never put the ice cream in the freezer. I'm really sorry." We exploded laughing.

Billy Joe's got his hand on the freezer and immediately quits cranking it. We come inside, and he goes, "Don't worry darling. We'll just have a milkshake." Everybody is really fucked up at that point, and Billy Joe picks up the big bowl of ice cream mixture, looks over to my husband, "You must be really proud of her," and starts to drink it. It all goes down the front of him and on the floor all over everything. Everybody is laughing. I was so embarrassed but too stoned to give a shit. At this point, Bucky and Billy are really drunk and get into Billy Joe's old sled of a giant car and do donuts in my big front yard. They just bounced through the ditch, knocked down the streets, and we're all still just laughing hysterically.

Billy Joe is a wild man, but he's always been really kind to me. There was a time when he'd been recording all day in my home studio, and *60 Minutes* was coming out to do a special on him. It just happened to be Easter, and I was having my bring-a-dish dinner that I always have. Then Dan Rather and *60 Minutes* showed up. I thought it was sweet and generous of Billy Joe to include me in something that was that important to him.

I've always loved "I Couldn't Be Me without You." "Together forever wherever we are, I couldn't be me without you." It doesn't get simpler than that, and it doesn't get truer. It's the beauty of his writing. I had the pleasure of singing a duet with Billy Joe on a song he wrote called "West Texas Waltz." I really love doing that song. I've never sat down and said, "I'm so inspired by Billy Joe, I'm going to do this." His influence is [through] osmosis.[5]

Kimmie Rhodes, born March 6, 1954, in Wichita Falls, Texas, began her career as a recording artist after moving to Austin, Texas, in 1979, where she partnered with Joe Gracey and Bobby Earl Smith, forming the band Kimmie Rhodes & the Jackalope Brothers. Rhodes recorded her first album at Willie Nelson's Pedernales Studios in Spicewood, Texas, in 1980, and she has released sixteen studio albums over the span of her career. Among the artists who have recorded her songs are Willie Nelson, Wynonna Judd, Trisha Yearwood, Amy Grant, Joe Ely, Waylon Jennings, and Emmylou Harris. In 1996, Rhodes appeared on an episode of Austin City Limits *with Willie Nelson, Waylon Jennings, Kris Kristofferson, and Billy Joe Shaver.*

Richie Allbright

I fell in love with music at a young age. I came to the understanding when I was nine that if someone was singing a song it didn't mean they wrote it. At the time, John Anderson's version of "I'm Just an Old Chunk of Coal (but I'm Gonna Be a Diamond Someday)" was a hit, and I had Johnny Rodriguez's first record [*Introducing*] that had "Ride Me Down Easy" on it. Rodriguez was first to record it, and on the that record the song was called "Easy Come, Easy Go." I guess they fixed the title later, when Bobby Bare did it. I got to sing the song with Johnny at his birthday bash a few years ago. It was me and my wife Kim, who does backing vocals for me, onstage with Johnny's band. Halfway through, Johnny came up. I just stepped out of the way with my guitar, and my wife sang backup with him. The crowd went crazy.

"I Couldn't Be Me without You" is a big favorite of mine. Johnny sang the song when Kim walked down the aisle at our wedding. Johnny, as

Richie Allbright. Photo by Kim Allbright.

much as I love him, sometimes forgets or just twists off, so I wasn't sure if he was going to show up. I had a backing track for him to sing to, but if he didn't show up I had the original recording as a backup plan. Fifteen minutes before, Johnny called me. He said, "Hey, man. It's Rodriguez. Is this the day you're supposed to be getting married?" "Yeah. It's today." He started laughing, "Man, I'm sitting on the street in a truck looking at you right now." My wife walked out the front door of the house and was standing on the porch. I was standing under a big oak tree and Johnny was ten feet away singing the song. When she [heard] Johnny start to sing, she [began] bawling. She had to pull herself together before she could come down the aisle and meet me under the oak. That song is so emotional. I relate to it. Before she came along, I was a huge mess. My life really turned around when I met her. "I Couldn't Be Me without You" is us. That's our relationship.

On my last album, *Back to Nashville*, the song "I Lived to Tell It All" is Shaver-like. It's the kind of thing I think he'd do, but he'd probably do it better. His songs set the bar. People like him and Roger Miller are so different in the way they write. It's almost like he's sitting at a bar, telling a story, just bullshitting with you. "I Live to Tell It All" is about leaving Texas for Nashville, with all the booze, drugs, being wasted, blowing it, and then coming back to Texas and starting over, saying, "I'm gonna get straight." Billy Joe's now influenced three generations. Everybody talks about originality, and I understand that, but I'm a believer that no matter who you are, you're a combination of your influences, and he's still out there going strong, inspiring a whole new generation of guys. It's crazy.[6]

Richie Allbright, born December 18, 1971, in Corpus Christi, was raised on a ranch outside of Mathis, Texas, where he fell in love with the music of Merle Haggard, Johnny Rodriguez, Gene Watson, Willie Nelson, and Waylon Jennings. In 1994, Allbright left Texas for Nashville where he spent fifteen years fighting the music business and his own demons. In 2008, he returned to Texas to record. He has released four albums and returned to Nashville to record his latest, the 2019 Aaron Rodgers–produced Back to Nashville.

Terri Hendrix

I was nineteen the first time I met Billy Joe. It would have been around 1999, at the Lake City Wine and Music Festival. He was playing solo. I was already a fan of his music. He shook my hand and looked me in the eyes, saying it was great to meet me. I've never had any extended conversations with him, but he's always been a complete gentleman. By the time he played, it was packed. We were out in the middle of the field, and it had all the telltale signs of getting rowdy. I was wondering how a

Terri Hendrix, Cheatham Street Warehouse, San Marcos, Texas, February 7, 2015. Photo by Brian T. Atkinson.

solo artist was going to be able to command attention, but he got up there like a preacher in the way he delivered and sang his songs and what he said in between them. People paid attention. No one was yucking it up when he was doing his show. He was a complete pro. It struck me because he was playing guitar unconventionally, the way he [made] chords. And the simplicity of [his] lyrics has such depth. It's simple at first, but it's complex. He writes free[ly] and without a lot of adjectives. He doesn't waste a single word. It made a lasting impression.

Townes was a little more on the floral side of poetry. Billy Joe's not a floral songwriter. Then you've got Guy Clark who is literal and did a lot of cowriting. "Boats to Build" [and] "Black Diamond Strings" are songs about objects. Billy Joe writes within the object and mixes different elements. With "Black Diamond Strings," it's an old style of storytelling. You're telling it to a crowd, not a party of one. Billy Joe is telling it to you, like he's in your ear and over a beer. That's what makes him special. "Love Is So Sweet" is such a simple song. He's talking to you when he sings, "Love is so sweet, it makes you dance when you walk down the street." He's telling somebody that might think they have it all [but] that they're missing the boat, because love is one of the best things you can have in life.

There are so many love songs that have been written, but for me that's not a love song. It's a reminding that contrasts him. His songs have a lot of light in them. He thinks about what I'm trying to say. He doesn't paint a picture; he makes a point. That's how I feel about him as a writer. His songs have a human element laced a little bit with religion, but he doesn't beat you over the head with [it]. I tend to get too wordy to try to explain something in a song rather than write better. Billy Joe Shaver didn't do that, because he writes so good. He doesn't sit there and mouth off about a topic. He's going to nail it right in.

Billy Joe's importance and significance have not been pumped up as much as other people. It's really important that a book like this be written, because he's been overlooked, and he's not out there promoting himself on Twitter, Facebook, and Instagram. Who knows where his masters are and [whether] his label will ever get all his stuff up to stream. That's what I worry about with people like him. How is his legacy going to last if the label doesn't keep it going, making sure his catalog is online? That stuff scares me, because he should have a legacy. What he lacked in education, he made up for as Beat Poet Laureate, grizzled as the Texas dirt. "Live Forever" is just as good a song as "This Land Is Your Land." He should be studied in English class.[7]

Terri Hendrix, born February 13, 1968 in San Antonio, is a Martindale, Texas–based singer-songwriter and multi-instrumentalist who made a name for herself with a unique blend of folk, pop, country, blues, and jazz beginning with her 1996 debut Two Dollar Shoes. *Hendrix won the Grammy for Best Country Instrumental Performance in 2002 for her Dixie Chicks co-write, "Lil' Jack Slade." In 2019, she released two recordings, the full-length* Talk to a Human *and the EP* Who Is Ann?

Chuck Mead (BR549)

The first time I met Billy Joe was around 1996 at 328 Performance Hall in Nashville. We [BR549] were doing a New Year's Eve show with Wayne "The Train" Hancock and Shaver when Eddy was still in the band. He knew we did "I Been to Georgia on a Fast Trian," but this was before we recorded it. I remember Billy Joe was unloading all his equipment out of the van. Some of the other guys were just standing around, and he was pumpin.' Billy Joe is a large man with presence. When he walks up onstage, you know he's lived it. He effortlessly draws upon his great catalog, and his shows are art. He commands the attention of the room. He's charismatic without trying to be. When you play a concert, particularly with him, it's like being at church with alcohol. When he's up there, he says, "That's the spark of God." My favorite thing he says onstage is, "God loves you when you dance." It's true.

Billy Joe has always been generous to me. He saved my ass one time at South by Southwest. We were doing this spot together, and I was supposed to go on, and he was supposed to go on after, but I got stuck in this horrible traffic on the other side of town. I was making calls, and Billy Joe said, "Well, shoot. I'll just go on before you to help the situation." He was willing to change a better spot with me, just because he's a sweet man.

I got to return the favor when we played the Exit/In in Nashville a few years ago. His van broke down. I tooled him around in our van, and we played with him. Just being able to talk with him, spend some time with

Chuck Mead. Photo by Joshua Black Wilkins.

him, you know you're close to a divine entity. I'm convinced that guys like him, Bob Dylan, Bill Monroe, Waylon, Willie, and Muddy Waters were really aliens with more alien DNA than the rest of us. All those guys influenced the way I write. You don't want to settle for second-best. I strive to tap into the ultimate truths of the human condition in an everyday language like Billy Joe does and wish that poetry fell out of my mouth all the time. It does on occasions, but guys like me have to work at it a little more.

I've been lucky to write with some of the greatest. I wrote with Guy Clark. There's a lot of sweat that goes into it. He and Billy are of the same ilk, of working hard to get it right. Every now and then, I tap into that inspiration that comes from being around and inspired by them. You want to actually talk about something instead of just saying, "Hey, let's write a song about screwing on the back of a pickup truck." If that really happened, you can say it in a way that doesn't come across as trite. It's a rare thing, and he can do it by standing there and talking. You can have a casual conversation, and these moments of brilliance come out. You don't know where it comes from. It's a gift. He can articulate things you feel in everyday language, without having the benefit of going to English 101, but he works at it. You can't have the great catalog he does without sitting down and having nuts and bolts, but the reality of it is, not everyone can just sit down and write a song. He's head and shoulders above most songwriters, and I appreciate the support and encouragement that he's given me anytime I was around him, treating me like I was just another guy out there tramping around telling my stories. He encouraged me to keep going. It's amazing. He's a stand-up guy. I wish that I'd written down some of our conversations, because I'd have a song. He's poetry in motion.[8]

Chuck Mead is a Kansas native who is best known for cofounding the esteemed nineties alt-country band BR5-49, which released seven albums and earned three Grammy nominations. Since then, he has released four solo albums and coproduced critically acclaimed tribute albums to Johnny Cash and Waylon Jennings. Mead acted as musical director, supervisor, and producer of the Broadway hit musical Million Dollar Quartet *and the companion CMT television show* Sun Records. *He recorded his last solo album,* Close to Home *at Sam Phillips Recording in Memphis.*

Tramp on Your Street

Jesse Dayton

I freaked out over *Tramp on Your Street* and started going to Billy Joe and Eddy's shows. The first time I met Billy Joe was in the bathroom at the Saxon Pub in Austin. I went up to him and said, "Hey, man, I like all that spiritual stuff you got going on in the songs." "Well, thank you, brother." "I grew up around some crazy Pentecostals in Beaumont, Texas." He busted out laughing, "Man, you are totally fucked then, aren't you?" "Yeah. My head's totally fucked." Later that night, I met Eddy. We were around the same age. I was on Justice Records, and about a year later I went to owner Randall Jamail and said, "I don't know what's going on with Billy Joe Shaver and Eddy, but you need to sign them." I was an advocate for them. I wouldn't shut up about them and how great they were.

When we were on the label, me and Eddy started hanging out, running around together, doing bad things and being naughty. We were best friends. I played with them at Willie's Picnic one time. We were in a trailer, and Sammy Allred pulled out a joint. I had a couple of puffs. Those guys finished it. I walk outside and go, "I gotta get back to bed," and I went back in and chilled out. There were a lot of nights like that with me and Eddy. We'd listen to Dickey Betts [of the Allman Brothers] and smoke dope. That's how it all got started. It was fucking awesome. The first time I partied with him, I played a biker show in San Antonio with Billy Joe and him and went onstage really drunk. I was unprofessionally drunk. I came offstage, and Billy goes, "You're not really holding your liquor too good today, are you?" "No, not really." "I thought it was a

Left to right: Jesse Dayton and Billy Joe Shaver. Photo courtesy of Hardcharger Music.

Left to right: Billy Joe Shaver shows his gold tooth to Jesse Dayton at LAX, Los Angeles, California, 2018. Photo courtesy of Hardcharger Music.

hell of a show." "Really?" "Yeah. You need to get hammered more before you go up there. I didn't know what was going to happen." I said, "Oh my God," because I thought for sure he'd say, "Hey, man, you got to pull your shit together." But we're playing a biker party, and it's rough as hell and he says, "I thought it was a great show," "Really? I thought I just shit the bed." "Well, I think you should party more, personally." I took it like a put down. Maybe he meant, "You're too stiff. You need to pull the stick out your ass." There's no telling what it meant, but what I'm going to remember is Billy Joe Shaver going, "I don't know, man. That was pretty damn good."

Eddy and I had parallels in our lives. He played a tour with Dwight Yoakam, and he filled in for Keith Anderson when Keith was producing one of my records. He'd made so much money off producing Dwight, he didn't really have to go on the road, so Eddy filled in. I talked to Dwight about it because I was playing in the band X in Los Angeles, and we did a bunch of shows. Dwight told me all about when Eddy was with him. I knew that the partying was going on. We were all partying. It was a crazy time. We were all young, ten feet tall, and bulletproof. If [the band Shaver] were in town, I would come party with them and their bass player, Keith Christopher, and the guys in the band would crash at my house when we were playing [Austin's] Continental Club or Saxon Pub. Eddy would unknowingly become a big influence on my guitar playing. You can hear Eddy Shaver's guitar on Waylon's [*Right for the Time*] record that I played on, because who you hang out with influences you.

I was shocked when Eddy died. I never thought he was going to take too much. It was weird. It was only three or four years that we were running around together, and then he died. I miss him a lot. If I think about it too much, I get upset. I showed up at the funeral, and Billy was meeting people up at the front. I walked up there, and he could tell that I was fixing to just bust out in tears, and goes, "Don't do it. I got all these people." He was basically telling me, "Don't come up here with that shit. I have to sit here and talk to all these people after you walk away." I said "okay"—and held it in. When I got out to my car, I cried for fifteen minutes because I was so shocked and upset.

Billy Joe became solemn after Eddy died. We wasn't as jokey, but he eventually broke through and accepted things for what they are. He's a real underdog, and he would give his last twenty bucks to some bum.

Left to right: Billy Joe Shaver and Eddy Shaver. Photo by C. J. Flanagan, courtesy of Keith Christopher archives.

He's not some asshole redneck. He has this world philosophy that very few guys have. It's profound. But even though he's a sweetheart—and I love him and would walk across of bed of coals and bail him out of jail in Bangkok—you wonder if anyone really knows him. He had such a hard childhood, and his life hasn't been easy. He bears so much in his songs it makes other people's songs sound trite and light. The fact that he gets knocked down and keeps getting up is unbelievable. I recorded with Cash, Waylon, Willie, Johnny Bush, Glen Campbell, Ray Price, but I don't think any of them have had a worse roll of dice than Billy. I'm sure some of it was brought on by Billy, but some of it was just bad luck. He used to tell me all the time, "Man, perfect lives make really boring songs."

Despite all his demons, Billy Joe's one of the most spiritual guys you'll ever be around. It's not right-wing redneck Christianity. Billy Joe's like Johnny Cash. There's an aura of spirituality around them. You can't explain it, but when you're with them you feel like you're closer to God. Billy Joe could represent people that are in a bad way because he knows what it's like, which is the same reason why Robin Williams would have to make people laugh. He knew what it was like to be really depressed. He's trying to release people of all their bullshit burdens. His philosophy is universal, and he's universally loved. I remember the night that he got arrested for shooting the guy. I was in the studio with Johnny Bush, and I go, "Billy Joe shot some motherfucker in his face." Johnny goes, "Really?" "Yeah. It's crazy, isn't it?" "What do you mean, Jess?" "What's he doing with a gun in a parking lot of a bar?" "Jess, we all carry guns." I thought to myself, *Oh, yeah. You guys are older. You're used to getting ripped off. You're all packing heat.*

I was recording with Waylon one time, and Billy came by. They hugged each other and didn't let go for about three minutes, which was almost uncomfortable for everybody else in the room. You would've thought they had just come back from a war. It was deep love, but then after five minutes it was, "All right, get the hell out of here, Hoss. I gotta get back to work." I ran into Billy Joe another time at LAX [airport], and he was showing me his gold tooth. I said, "Hey, man, if you're from Mexia, and you get a goddamn gold tooth it's like hitting the lottery." He just loved that. He was laughing his ass off.[1]

Jesse Dayton, born in Beaumont, Texas, is an Austin -based singer-song-writer and musician best known for his guitar work with Johnny Cash, Waylon Jennings, and Willie Nelson as well as the Supersuckers and Kris Kristofferson. Dayton has recorded twelve solo albums, including Jesse Sings Kinky, *which he released after playing Friedman in the stage play* Becoming Kinky. *In 2014, Dayton toured with legendary cowpunk singer John Doe. In 2016, he released his ninth album,* The Revealer, *on his Hardcharger Records imprint through Blue Élan Records.*

Keith Christopher

I first met Billy Joe Shaver in the [late] eighties in Nashville. I just moved there from Atlanta and was new to the underground rock scene. I was getting to know people. They said, "You gotta see this guy, Billy Joe Shaver, and his son's an incredible guitar player." I saw them at a small club. Eddy had a ten-thousand-watt Mesa/Boogie amp head. It was like a Marshall rock and roll set with four-twelve cabinets turned to the wall. He put blankets over it, and it was still loud as fuck. Then there's Billy Joe. I thought, *Who the hell are these guys?* They were so unique. I never

Left to right: Billy Joe Shaver and Keith Christopher. Photo by Mark Miks, courtesy of Keith Christopher archives.

saw anything like it before. It was the most incredible thing I'd heard. Eddy was extra showing off that night because he'd heard of my band the Georgia Satellites and knew I was there. I met them in the bathroom. We did coke. It was common back then. I left Atlanta because of all the coke, but Nashville was every bit as good. I wound up replacing their bass player and was with Billy Joe until Eddy's death in 2000.

Everyone was scared to death of Billy Joe, and Eddy looked mean. People were horrified. Billy Joe had a reputation for knocking people out. People would get drunk and challenge him. They wanted to see how bad he really was. They were really fucking with him, which was a bad idea. Billy Joe's a big, scary, strong dude with [huge] arms and a reach longer than Muhammad Ali. We were at Third Coast in Nashville, and David Briggs was there. He was an area loudmouth, drunk on tequila, and popping off to Billy. Billy Joe kept saying, "Leave me alone. Back off." David was fine to leave, but he kept mouthing off. Billy Joe reached down and took off his flip-flops. He hit David so hard, he broke his jaw, busted his face, and knocked him over two tables with one punch. He put his flip-flops back on, and we left. I was thoroughly impressed.

We used to drive in Billy Joe's pieced-together van all the time. The driver's seat was broken. He had a spare tire in the back to hold it up, and we'd have to fix the engine. One time, we were driving and saw flames coming out. Billy Joe pulled over and fixed it with coat hangers and cardboard. When we were on tour with Willie Nelson, we'd follow his bus. They're all sleeping in the bus, and we're driving all night. We'd show up to a gig and open the door. Cigarette smoke comes out, McDonald's bags fall out, and we roll out in our travel clothes, get dressed in the parking lot, get onstage, and kick major ass.

When I moved to Austin, I lived in the hills with Billy Joe, Eddy, and Brenda. It was insane. Brenda was insane. She was funny, loud, and talked nonstop. Eddy looked identical to her. Both of them would run Billy Joe ragged. We were all doing speed at the time. Willie's crew got us going. They had connections to get unbelievably pure and insanely strong shit. We would be up for days. We were in the van one time driving around some city with Eddy playing in the back. We were having a good time and didn't want to go back to the hotel. So we drove around the perimeter for hours, singing, drinking, and having fun.

We drove all the way to a gig in Raleigh, and Billy Joe was speeding with a trailer. We got pulled over, and they took him to jail. We went on to the gig without him. They didn't know who we were. "You guys aren't booked. We have someone else playing tonight." We thought, *Oh, man,* and we went to get Billy Joe out of jail. One of the policemen was a big David Allan Coe fan. He finally recognized Billy Joe and said, "You wouldn't happen to be Billy Joe, would you?" "Yes, sir. I am. Me and David Allan Coe go way back." "Yes, sir, I know." He turns and says, "Get this man out of jail right now!" Billy Joe gave him some CDs, and we left. When we got to [the venue] we said, "Billy, we're not playing here tonight." He said, "What? Wait here." He went inside, and a few minutes later he came back out and said, "Let's load in." He threatened the guy, grabbed him, choked him, and was going to punch him. We ended up playing, and the scheduled band opened for us. We got paid and drove off. Just another day at the office.

Billy Joe was good like that. We always got paid. He kept us working. He was very fair with money. As long as you did the gig, he didn't care what else you did. You can't be messed up onstage. Well, we were, but all on the same level. Billy Joe was always dedicated to what he was doing. He was totally committed to performing and his unbelievable storytelling. He really believed in his songs. He put everything he had into it, and it came across. People would cry at shows. It was my favorite band. Real deal and from the heart. It's a rare thing.

We went to Australia with Willie on the Spirit Tour [in support of his 1996 *Spirit* album]. Willie had a smaller band. They were doing it like *Unplugged* [on MTV], but Willie started adding one person at a time back in, so it ended up being the full band anyway. We were there playing this big theater to a room of blue-tops: fancy old people that put a blue tint to their hair. It was weird. We were doing a serious song. Billy Joe's praying and putting his heart into it. Someone yells, "Where's Willie?" Billy Joe got up to the mic, "If he was up your ass you'd know where he was!" Everybody [in the audience] made the "Oh no! Mr. Bill!" mouth. We had trouble winning that audience back over.

We were in Sydney on the east coast with Willie and Waylon [and then flew] on a small plane [across Australia] to Perth. Waylon has a phobia about small planes [because he was supposed to be on Buddy Holly's plane that crashed]. When the plane [taxied] up, Waylon didn't like the looks of it. They ordered another plane, and our huge entourage waited several hours at the bar. I'm sure we drank them dry. When the plane finally came, everybody was really sauced. We started to board, and I was behind Billy Joe. Waylon was in front of him, with Jessi Colter, and Willie in front of him. We're going up the stairs, and right as Waylon's going on, Billy Joe started singing "Chantilly Lace" by the Big Bopper [who took Waylon's place on Buddy's plane]. Everyone was already pissed [that we'd] had to wait all day, and Waylon turned around swinging. "I'm gonna kill you!" Billy had his hands on Waylon's shoulder blades so Waylon couldn't turn around. He's trying to push him on the plane while Waylon's reaching back to hit him. Willie stepped in and stopped it. It was the best thing I've seen. Billy Joe just loved fucking with people. That's part of the reason he doesn't get the credit he should. He does crazy shit he shouldn't do.

I was in the front seat of the van when Billy Joe wrote "Live Forever." Eddy was in the back with Craig Wright who played drums. We're driving, and Billy Joe says, "Tear me off a piece of that McDonald's sack." He called it a sack, not a bag. I tore off a piece, and he started writing the song on it. He handed it to me and said, "Can you add anything to this? Take a verse." He was really good about including everyone. I read the lyrics and thought, *Holy fuck, man. I can't add anything to this.*

Recording with Billy Joe was weird. It could be good or not. I have this glossy memory of everything being great, but he could be difficult because he couldn't count. He didn't have any musical knowledge to explain what he wanted. He just knew what he didn't want. He and Eddy used to bicker. Eddy would get him upset for fun. They picked at each other a lot. They were very competitive. There was always a fight about the volume of Eddy's guitar, and Eddy would do things to instigate a big blowout. Billy would say, "Eddy, you little dickhead." It was tense, a weird relationship. They tried to blow each other offstage and steal the spotlight. That's why the shows were so great. I went to Eddy's funeral when he died. Billy Joe stood next to the casket, shook people's hands, and thanked them for coming. It was hard. Billy Joe would have done anything for Eddy.[2]

Keith Christopher, born September 17, 1954, in Atlanta, cofounded the southern rock band Keith and the Satellites in 1980 alongside Dan Baird, Rick Richards, and Davis Michaelson. Later known as the Georgia Satellites, the band is best known for their 1986 single "Keep Your Hands to Yourself," which went to number two on the Billboard Hot 100. *After departing the group, Christopher recorded on two of Baird's solo efforts,* Love Songs for the Hearing Impaired (1992) *and* Buffalo Nickel (1996). *Christopher spent six years in the nineties touring with Billy Joe Shaver and played on the albums* Tramp on Your Street (1993), Unshaven (1995), *and* Electric Shaver (1999). *Christopher was a member of the Kenny Wayne Shepard Band in the 2000s and played on Shepard's 1999 album* Live On. *His credits also include Steve Marriott and Humble Pie, Aaron Lee Tasjan, Todd Snider, and the Brains, whose song "Money Changes Everything" became a hit for Cyndi Lauper in 1984. He is currently a member of legendary southern rock band Lynyrd Skynyrd.*

David Waddell

I discovered Billy Joe Shaver's music in 1971 when I was seventeen. My uncle Frank Waddell got a new copy of Kris Kristofferson's *The Silver Tongued Devil and I.* Our favorite song on that record was and still is "Good Christian Soldier." We thought, *Who the hell is this Billy Joe Shaver?* I never forgot the song. It just kept ringing in my head for years

David Waddell tour poster. Photo by Courtney S. Lennon.

and made me a fan. He has these beautiful hooks and melodies that cross between country and blues. It made me more a fan of him than Kris, I'm sorry to say. He's straight to the point, and everything he writes comes from his own experiences. He believes in what he writes and is honest. He's the General Patton of the outlaw country movement.

Never in a million years would I have pictured myself playing bass for and singing harmony with the very same dude who wrote "Good Christian Soldier." I started out in Billy's band when me and my brother Leland were with [singer] Pat McLaughlin at a bar down on Second Avenue in Nashville opening for Billy. After the gig, he asked us to go to New York with him. I thought, *Man, it's Billy Joe Shaver, the most respected songwriter in Nashville.* At the time, Pat's band was the hottest in town, but my heart triple-beat when Billy Joe asked the Waddell Brothers to join his band. Getting the gig with him really raised me up the ladder of success with the most influential, powerful, important songwriters and record companies on Music Row. Billy Joe worked all the time and paid his musicians well. There was a time when he fired me and gave me severance pay. Next week, he hired me back with a raise. I said, "I ain't giving your severance money back!" "Good, then I won't have to pay you the next time I fire you."

We used to ride around in his van, and we'd run into issues. There was the time when we were driving in the freezing cold, way up north in a blizzard, and the heater quit. I rolled down the electric window, and it wouldn't go back up. We almost froze to death on that one. Another time driving in the same van, going across the desert to California in the summer, it started overheating so we had to run the heater the whole way to keep the motor from burning up. We almost died of heat stroke, and Eddy said, "Daddy, drop me off at the Albuquerque airport. I'm dying. I'm flying the rest of the way." When we played a gig in Atlanta, we had the night off and Eddy asked me if I wanted to go party. I got duded up, shaved, and was ready to find some girls and have a few drinks. We drove to town, pulled into a parking lot in a huge mall, and walked a mile to this place Eddy said was "really super" ("and they have good cold beer"). We finally found it. It turned out to be a Chuck E. Cheese.

One time we stopped off in Vegas after a California tour and lost all our money in three days and nights. Billy Joe came to my room and asked how much I won. I'd just gotten dressed and heard a chink-chink-

chink sound. Black casino chips had slipped into the lining of my old leather jacket from a hole in the pocket. We cashed them in, bought peanut butter, jelly, and a loaf of white bread, filled up with gas, and hit the road. When we got to back to Waco, Billy said to me, "David, I am gonna blame this whole dang mess on you when I talk to Brenda." I said, "Man, ain't that what you do every time?" "Yes, sir, that's one of the good things about having you in the band."

Billy Joe set me straight in the right direction as a songwriter. He told me to write what I know and gave me the self-confidence I needed. He told me a million times, "David, man, you need to quit being a sideman and sing. Front your own band and do your own songs." I played with him one last time at the Grand Ole Opry and did just that. He's a hero to me.[3]

David Waddell, born in 1953, in Orangeburg, South Carolina, started his career playing bass and singing in nightclubs on the Chitlin' Circuit in the South. In 1972 he moved to Austin, Texas, opening shows for Johnny Winter. In 1976, he went to Nashville where he played with Billy Joe Shaver, Townes Van Zandt, Willie Nelson, and the Carter Family. He then began writing his own songs and working for publishing houses on Music Row. In 1997, after the death of his friend Van Zandt, he coproduced the scattershot archival Van Zandt recording In The Beginning *for Compadre records. Waddell currently lives in Konstanz, Germany, where he fronts the outlaw country blues group David Waddell & Hellbound Train.*

Rosie Flores

Billy Joe Shaver is a step above with Bob Dylan, a tough-as-nails, no-bullshit cowboy who tells it like it is and won't put up with anybody trying to pull wool over his eyes. When *Tramp on Your Street* came out, I pretty much lived and breathed it. I learned to play all the songs. Shaver [the band] weren't wimpy. They [incorporated] country and hard rock elements. I loved Eddy on guitar. He brought that "We're here to melt your face off and show you some great songs, we're not going to pussyfoot around it, we're gonna rock" [attitude]. Billy Joe is what he appears to be and brings in sadness with a sharp-witted poet's mind. When I'm around him, I always get the feeling that he's thinking in that world.

Rosie Flores backstage at Ameripolitan Awards, Memphis, Tennessee, February 25, 2019. Photo by Mark Whitfield Lennon.

He won't talk about boring things or people personally. He talks about interesting things he's run across. I heard him defend himself when he shot that guy. "I did not say 'Where do you want it?'" he said, "but the guy kept following me, trying to pick a fight. I had a gun, pointed it at him, and shot him." He sets it straight. I would have done the same.

I first met Billy Joe in the nineties when we were on three tours in Europe, and we've played together at places in Nashville like the Exit/In through the years. We'd run into him and Eddy at the dining room breakfast table [in Europe]. We liked bringing Texas songwriters over there, just hanging out and joking around. He's a real Texas gentleman with a sweet side, and he's always treated me with the utmost respect. He treats me like a brother and gives me a little shit here and there. He's somebody who could grab your head and give you a noogie. He's endearing, charming, and always teasing me. Eddy always had something great to say about my guitar playing. People didn't even know I played guitar back in those days. Even when my songs were getting airplay on the radio, no one would say "That's Rosie Flores on guitar." Eddy paid attention, and Billy Joe always said, "My son loves the way you play guitar." Billy Joe's always got a great guitar player, but I'd love to step in and play with his band.

When Billy Joe performs, he pulls you in and gives you the chills with songs like "Live Forever" and "I'm Just an Old Chunk of Coal (but I'm Gonna Be a Diamond Someday)." He wants you to get what he's saying. His delivery is truthful and reaches the audience. He's inside the song and will spread his arms out like an eagle, pull you into his heart, and make sure that you understand every word he's singing. He's great with enunciation, and his voice comes across. You're not gonna get do-wa-diddy with him. He's gonna find something that expresses what's going on in his heart and soul. He puts time into the song. I strive to write songs like that. You have guys like Billy Joe and Dave Alvin, [for whom] it comes so easy. It's amazing.

Billy Joe never turned into a big star, because not everyone's meant to do the big star thing. You have to be willing to put up with bullshit. There's promotion and press, and you have to work really hard. Record labels give you a list that doesn't guarantee you're going to make it to the rock star level. Billy Joe won't play the game. He's with Johnny Cash, Townes Van Zandt, and Willie Nelson as the four presidents of great songwriting. Their faces should be carved into Mount Rockmore so we can look at them historically as the songwriters who made their mark, and in fifty years young artists can look up to them and know who to aspire to be.[4]

Rosie Flores, born September 10, 1950, in San Antonio, began playing the San Diego nightclub circuit as a member of Rosie and the Screamers. Flores then joined the cowpunk band Screamin' Sirens before releasing her 1987 self-titled debut. Flores is an award-winning singer-songwriter and guitarist who toured with rockabilly legend Wanda Jackson during the mid-nineties rockabilly revival and spent time as a member of Asleep at the Wheel in 1997.

Brian Molnar

The first time I saw Billy Joe was in the late nineties when I was in college. It was at this old theater in Williamsport, Pennsylvania. There wasn't an opener listed on the ticket. When I got there, I saw Billy Joe was opening with Eddy. I couldn't believe it. My head just about exploded. During the show, Billy would pick up a guitar to start things off, but for the most part, it was Eddy following him around playing this rhythm and lead stuff. Eddy blew my mind. I don't think I've heard a better guitar player. Even as a guitar player, I don't know how he did it all at once. There was a salt-of-the-earth genuineness to what they did, which was greater than the sum of its parts. The purity of what they do, and the way it touches the soul, is mind-boggling. Billy Joe has it in his voice, and Eddy had it in his fingers. They were fantastic together. Pure magic. It was one of the best shows I've seen, and afterward I went and saw Billy Joe any chance I got. I've seen him so many times, I can't remember how many.

I got to know Billy Joe through Kinky Friedman. I've never been with both of them in a room at the same time, but I've worked with Kinky for a long time. I met Kinky at a little house concert here in New Jersey. I don't think anybody remotely my age in this part of the world was as familiar with his stuff. I asked him some really intelligent questions that made his eyebrows go up. He said, "Look man, I'm really tired, but if you're ever in Texas, look me up. We'll continue the conversation then." So I booked some Texas shows and called him. He didn't remember me, but he said, "I must have liked you." We went back and forth like that. I went down there and called him. He didn't answer or call me back. At the end of the tour, I tried him one last time.

He picked up the phone, was chipper, and said, "Sorry. I've been depressed. My dog died. I'm in a terrible state. Why don't you come stay a couple days?" I thought we were going to get a beer. I got there, and he said, "I don't remember you at all. You're not who I thought you were." I spent the next day asking questions, but he wouldn't really talk. I thought, He's just not in the mood for this. I kept asking about his music, and he found this CD of demos with his name on it. He had this beat-to-hell CD radio, and couldn't get the CD in. He didn't realize it had tracks from his second album in the seventies. He heard them and lit up telling me about the recording process with Willie Nelson and Leon

Left to right: Brian Molnar and Billy Joe Shaver, Willie Nelson's Fourth of July Picnic, Austin360 Amphitheater, Del Valle, Texas, 2016. Photo by Tierney Wiles, courtesy of Brian Molnar.

Russell. Then they sent him to Los Angeles to get a slick producer and cut stuff out of the songs. He was happy at the end, and I thought, This is the moment of truth. I said, "Do you want to hear anything of mine?" The cigar fell out of his mouth. "Fuck, no. I'm sure it's going to suck. I haven't heard anything good in thirty-five years, but since you're here, I guess I gotta listen to it. I don't go for this hootenanny shit. If you've got a CD, put it in, and I'll listen to three songs. Then, I'm going to read this [Winston] Churchill book and go to sleep." I was mortified.

I went to my room and got the CD. He didn't say anything as it played. It got to the end, and he pulled out his cigar, looked at me, jumped up and said, "That's the best thing I've heard in thirty-five years! I love it!"

We stayed up all night planning tours, and the rest is history. We've been together for nine years now. My role changes from time to time. If I'm with him on the road, I open all the shows and road-manage. I design the merch, sell it, and drive the truck from show to show. I produced his last two studio albums, as well as a bunch of live ones. I'm also his archivist. When we need something, we do a tape transfer and pull it off.

Kinky never formally introduced me to Billy Joe, but whenever I go see him Kinky will say, "My friend Brian's coming to the show. Look out for him." I've helped run the merch for Billy Joe if he didn't have someone there. He's completely genuine and exactly what you'd expect. It's not an act onstage. It's him. He really loves his audience. I don't think anybody I've been around is as loyal to their audience and loves them that much, with maybe the exception of Willie.

I was running merch for Billy Joe in Manhattan. He's beaming, smiling, signing autographs for everybody, and having a great time. Finally, he said, "I love all of you. Everybody pick something you want and take it home. It's on me." I said, "Are you serious, man? You drove all the way here for this one gig, and you're gonna give it all away?" "Brian, it's only money. It'll go away." I was touched. He moves a room, and you can't help but feel that wherever he's going, he's bringing everybody with him. He can change [an] audience. Everybody was so excited, and so was he, just smiling and hugging people. I'd never seen a performer do that. It wasn't about the money. It was about the people, communicating with them and having a mutual experience. He's the same way every time I've seen him. I've felt it. It's about getting to perform, share his songs, and share his life with people. I don't know a more genuine person. I think that's why those songs come out of him. He's pure Billy Joe. There's no other way to put it, but I wouldn't want to be a club owner ripping him off.

The greatest thing about Billy Joe's songwriting is that he says so much, so deeply, and in such a simple way. It doesn't have to be complicated to say a very complicated thing. I don't know a lot of songwriters who can do that. There's no question what he's talking about. It's a deep human experience every time. He's not vague. He's to the point and says things in a way that everyone can relate to. There's not a song that isn't like that. "I'm Just an Old Chunk of Coal (but I'm Gonna Be a Diamond Someday)" is simple, but doesn't that say it all? It's what every human being who is trying to be better is trying to do. It'd take Bob Dylan at least seven minutes to get that one line out. That's the genius of Billy Joe. He can distill it down to pure moonshine. It's the real thing.

I hope to someday write a song as good as anything he's done. I hope to be as moving onstage as he can be in any condition. That's one of the most important things a performer can do. It's the weird X factor that's between the lines of the song and performance. The soul of it. It's a good thing we all haven't had to live the hard life he has, and we're lucky to have him to communicate it to us and for us.

Billy Joe, Townes Van Zandt, Guy Clark, Kris Kristofferson, and Kinky Friedman took the country genre and added a new level of depth. Billy Joe spearheaded it. It doesn't matter if people know who he is. He's effected country songwriting and brought it up a level from the first time his songs were recorded. He set a new benchmark for country songwriting, and it hasn't gotten any better. Nobody's brought it a step further than he has. Billy Joe is a genius natural songwriter. Great artists spend time trying to figuring out how to speak the truth. He's so good at conveying it in as few words as possible. That's where guys like Bob Dylan look up to him, and me and Kinky or anybody else who tried to write after hearing his songs. He set a new standard.[5]

Brian Molnar, born January 19, 1978, in Edison, New Jersey, is a singer-songwriter and record producer who has released several albums, including the number-one roots country album Of the Fall. *Brian has toured extensively with Kinky Friedman and produced his albums* The Loneliest Man I Ever Met *and* Circus of Life. *He is the cofounder of Avenue A Records, which also released Friedman's 2013 album,* Lost and Found: The Famous Living Room Tape.

Radney Foster

I became aware of Billy Joe Shaver's music and songwriting in high school from *Honky Tonk Heroes*. It was so cool that Waylon thought, *I love this songwriter so much, I'm going to do an album of his songs.* The first time I heard John Anderson's "I'm Just an Old Chunk of Coal (but I'm Gonna Be a Diamond Someday)" I thought, *Who is this singer? What the heck is that?* Then I said, "Ah, Billy Joe wrote that song. That makes

Radney Foster backstage before at show at Happy Days Lodge, Cuyahoga Valley National Park, Peninsula, Ohio, March 16, 2018. Photo by Mark Whitfield Lennon.

sense." I'm drawn to the absolute poetry of his lyrics. It has that flowery descriptiveness yet it never loses that country boy conversationality. "When Jesus Was Our Savior and Cotton Was Our King," and "Honky Tonk Heroes" are amazing songs. They are brilliant and way past anything.

I met Eddy Shaver before I met Billy Joe. We were on tour together when he was playing in Dwight Yoakam's band and I was in Foster & Lloyd. Eddy was very funny. He was a bombastic guy. Larger than life. He was crazy-hearted and loved playing guitar like crazy. I told him that I'd never met his dad, but that he was legendary to me and I was a fan. I think about that generation of songwriters: Guy Clark, Billy Joe, and Harlan Howard. I got to write with all of them. They all had incredible craftsman skills, but each had a little different approach. Guy was always more concerned with the art of it. You knew your goal with Guy was making a piece of art and that the possible by-product [might] be a hit song and a fan favorite that would lift your heart and spirit. Maybe it would grab you and make you kiss your sweetheart.

Harlan was more structured. The goal was writing a hit song. It needed to be worth a damn as a song and say something, but the goal was to write a hit. With Billy Joe, it was somewhere in between. You had the art side you [had] with Guy, but you had the Harlan Howard side. With Billy Joe, I'd throw out a line, and he'd say, "That's good, but people don't talk that way. Let's make it how people really would talk." You don't want the conversation to be the way people talk. You want it to sound like how you wish people talk but still have that straight-ahead earthiness.

After I went solo, I wrote a song with Billy Joe. It was around 1996. Billy Joe and Eddy had an apartment they were sharing in Nashville, and they were in the band Shaver. The song was called "It Doesn't Mean a Thing," which is about a woman who is out on the town right after her man left. It was great writing with him. He was probably around the age I am now, late fifties, and I was in my early thirties. There's something about that twenty years more of writing that brings a level of acumen that keeps growing. In his case, it certainly did. He knew so many effortless ways to flip things around, say it differently, and move the ball forward from a pure craftsmanship level. The song was pretty good, and it got in contention to be recorded for my next record, but it was right before I got remarried and around the time I had an album rejected by Arista that never came out.

Billy Joe's greatest strength as a performer is his charisma and ability to get lost in whatever world he's in. I've watched him drop to his knees and pray in the midst of a performance and have so much rock and roll swagger it's not even funny. The last time I saw him was two years ago at Larry Joe Taylor's [Music Festival]. He brought the house down. It was unbelievable to see a guy in his late seventies rocking it and kicking ass.

There's the public persona and the private man, which are often two different things, but I think Billy Joe is what he is. His ultimate legacy is going to be his songs. It's not going to be the wild characteristics or that he shot some guy. It's the songs and the stories behind them. Billy Joe went to top of the cliffs at the Harpeth River in Nashville. He was going to kill himself. He prayed, "Lord give me one reason not to end it all," and wrote "I'm Just an Old Chunk of Coal (but I'm Gonna Be a Diamond Someday)" right there. Like many artists, he's always dealt with manic-depressive issues. I think that's what makes [great] writers and painters. We all tend to use art as a mechanism for staying alive and [coping] with it. I think the cool part about his surge as a performer was starting a band with Eddy. It's one of the coolest things in the world. In late middle age he starts a band with his son, who is a wizard guitar player, and combines his own lyricism with the rock and roll tinge Eddy brought to it. I think it helped Billy Joe reinvent himself. I can't imagine what he went through when Eddy died. That would be my worst nightmare. I don't want to survive my children.[6]

Radney Foster, born July 20, 1959, in Del Rio, Texas, began his recording career as one half of the duo Foster & Lloyd ("Crazy Over You," "Texas in 1880"). Foster embarked on his solo career with his 1992 album Del Rio, TX 1959, *which featured his iconic songs "Just Call Me Lonesome" and "Nobody Wins." Foster's songwriting melds the Texas singer-songwriter style with a pop edge. His songs have been recorded by Keith Urban ("Raining on Sunday") and Dierks Bentley ("Sweet and Wild"), and he has collaborated with fellow Texas artists like Randy Rogers ("Dancing the Dark"). Foster's 2017 album* For You to See the Stars *is a collection of songs that correspond to the short stories in his book of the same title.*

Bruce Robison

Billy Joe Shaver redefined country music. He's the gold standard of poetic purity, a songwriter's songwriter with unvarnished emotional complexity and fearless expression that people gravitate toward. He's laser-focused, with incredible identity within himself, testifying, proselytizing, and spreading the word in beer joints and honky-tonks. No one else would do that. The first time I saw Billy Joe was in Nashville when Eddy was still alive. He was a little too loud for me. I was really wanting to hear Billy Joe's songs, but it was an amazing combo, and Billy Joe dropped to his knees testifying. I was thinking, *How lucky am I to see that?* He's incredibly real. It jumps out in Nashville, where everybody's phony. Billy Joe is the opposite. Nobody's called him phony in his life.

Left to right: Bruce Robison and Kent Finlay, Texas Music Theater, San Marcos, Texas, April 27, 2014. Photo by Brian T. Atkinson.

We did a show together in Rockport, [Texas,] a year after Eddy died. The guys in his band were all friends of mine and congratulating me on my first child. Billy Joe came up, told me to prize the moment, and said a prayer. It was beautiful for him to tell me how happy he was for me when his heart was breaking from the loss of his son. It was hard for me to not be overcome by emotion, but he wasn't going to let that stop him from being in that moment.

Kelly Willis and I did *A Tribute to Billy Joe Shaver (Live)* and picked "Ride Me Down Easy" because it's brilliant. I do a lot of tributes and wanted to do something not so obvious and have Kelly sing. There was no harmony on it normally. We sang it well. I love that song. It's crazy poetry, raised atop a mountain. Richie [Albright of the Waylors] said he would play drums with [Kelly and me] that night, so the drummer we brought isn't on it. Bobby Bare did the hit version in quarter time, but Billy Joe always did it as a waltz, and we did it as a waltz. It's rare to have a song that can work in a completely different time signature.

I count Billy Joe as a friend, but I've always been a little intimidated by him because he's a powerful person. [He's] this legendary figure that was such a big part of Waylon finding his way, and he almost got beat up intimidating Waylon. Billy Joe shows up and says, Do this, do this. Nobody has done anything like that as a songwriter. Never in a million years, and the crazy thing is, the songs are differential, strong, and clear. Hearing [*Honky Tonk Heroes*] the first time was a big moment for me. It's one of the top-five strongest albums in country music. I've listened to his songs a million times, completely inspired. Songs like "Black Rose" or "Honky Tonk Heroes" are what I want to do—simple, clear, sparse, and beautiful songs. Billy Joe is a guy that spends years out in a minivan drinking Red Bull and making it to the next show. People will be singing songs like "I Been to Georgia on a Fast Train" forever because they make everybody feel good, and you can play it to a train beat to pick up your show. So, until idiots move to Mars, his songs will be around. He's an icon. He's never going away.[7]

Bruce Robison, born June 11, 1966, grew up in Bandera, Texas, alongside his singer-songwriter brother Charlie Robison ("New Year's Day") and sister Robyn Ludwick ("Wimberly Strong"). Robison has written several number-one hits, including Faith Hill and Tim McGraw's "Angry All the Time" (2001) and the Dixie Chicks song "Travelin' Soldier" (2003). Robison has released nine solo albums, beginning with his 1996 self-titled debut, and four collaborations with wife and fellow singer-songwriter Kelly Willis, two of which—Cheater's Game (2013) and Our Year (2014)—reached the top forty on the Billboard Top Country Albums chart. The duo perform "Ride Me Down Easy" on the 2007 album A Tribute to Billy Joe Shaver (Live).

Jeremy Lynn Woodall

I first heard Billy Joe Shaver on *Headbangers Ball* on MTV, a heavy metal program that showed videos after school. That was long before I met

Billy. I didn't put two and two together until I had been playing with him for a little while. He's a great and giving person. He used to come out and watch [my band Diamondback TX] play and became a fan. He'd get up and jam with us sometimes. Eddy too. He'd get up and play with us all night. That's how I got to know those two. Then one thing led to another, and he asked me to come play for him [after Eddy died]. I love playing his music, but the thing I enjoy the most is his friendship and stories. Traveling with him is like traveling with a president because he's so loved and connected. He's a big piece of history in the places we go.

I grew up learning country and rock and ended up playing both in my life. Billy Joe Shaver was the perfect marriage of what I was doing and what country was. For a punk rocker like me to end up playing in what some people would call an old-school country band is unheard of, but it's ice cream and cookies. It comes naturally to me. I think that's the reason Billy Joe picked me to be in his band. I was playing in a country band to actually make money, and he enjoyed the way I play. I feed off people enjoying my guitar playing. I love it. I was very fortunate to be able to go and play for him, and I still wake up and pinch myself. I will never take it for granted because of the caliber of writer he is.

The very first time I ever played for Billy Joe was at a birthday party at a little steakhouse. We sat down at a booth before soundcheck, and I started picking at him about songwriting. There's not much we could cover, but he did tell me to write songs that are easy for people to figure out and not hard to listen to. Write songs with meaning and purpose that take you somewhere. I took that to heart. I thought, *Let's keep it simple. [Write] something people are familiar with, so they understand, and it feels like home.* I've kept with that motif and ended up writing a song that was directly influenced by him called "House on the Hill." It's been performed by several bands. To say that he's been an influence on me would be a huge understatement.

The reason I enjoy Billy Joe so much is because we're both still kids at heart and enjoy a rainbow: "Hey, look over there, that's beautiful." That's what Billy Joe sees, and that's what he writes about as opposed to some political garbage. If Billy Joe had an essence, it would be sunset or a mountaintop seen from a plane. Those things are beautiful, and he still draws from it. It's a child-like quality that he's lucky he's held on to. He sees through the negative and always grabs on to the positive. He's

Jeremy Lynn Woodall performing at the City Winery, Nashville, Tennessee. Photo by Kathy Reid-Papson.

not jaded. We've talked miles and miles about it. I don't think he would agree that his songs help people as much as I [think they] do, but he's a great healing writer, and his songs can do anybody good.

We were playing Bowling Green, Kentucky, one night, and the opening band came on and did a great set. The crowd was really involved. That's good. We like that. When we climbed onstage, the drummer counted off "I Been to Georgia on a Fast Train." Then the lights went out. A storm knocked out the electricity. People started lighting up their cell phones. Billy Joe looked at me, and I looked at him. We went to the middle of the audience, and they got an impromptu concert with Billy Joe and no electricity. Just him singing to three hundred people. When I'm lying on my death bed, I'll always think back to that night with the rain beating down on the roof with Billy Joe Shaver singing his heart out. It was magical. One in a million. There hasn't been another one like it.

Billy Joe carries a charisma that's hard to put your finger on. He doesn't need a band. He doesn't need a guitar player. He doesn't even need a guitar. He can walk up onstage and entertain you for ninety minutes with just him and a microphone, telling stories and singing to you. He's going to allow you in, and you're going to allow him in. It's very rare. It's an agreement between him and his fans. I hate to say it, but you see a lot of artists put up a wall between them and their audience. Not to be cliché, but [look at] Pink Floyd. It happens. There's years and years of rock stardom to back up that point. You know how rock stars act. Billy Joe is so against the wall, it's refreshing. He comes from a time where [rock stardom] wasn't a thing. I think a lot of people can identify with that, but if a million people don't, it doesn't matter, he's having a great time doing what he does. It's a beautiful thing, and, as his guitar player, I know that I'm unnecessary. I'm very lucky and humbled to be there.

Honky Tonk Heroes hit the nail right on the head. The melding of Billy Joe's songs and Waylon performing them was the lightning bolt for the outlaw movement. At the time, even Willie Nelson was doing what they wanted in Nashville, but once Billy Joe put pen to paper and brought those songs to Waylon, the movement began. [There are] people who would disagree with me on that, but if you look back, you can tell it was that album that put it on the map. Without Billy Joe, it would have just [lain] there throughout the seventies. You would have had some mediocre albums. Those other people are all just stragglers. I can prove it. Listen to any band that's out there today calling themselves *outlaw*. Billy Joe set the bar. It's a tough bar to [get over]. There are a lot of people who tried, but it still hasn't been done.[8]

Jeremy Lynn Woodall is a singer-songwriter from Central Texas who was handpicked by Eddy Shaver to replace him in Billy Joe Shaver's band while Woodall was a member of the group Diamondback TX. Woodall was then lead guitarist of Shaver's band for fifteen years. He appeared on the albums A Tribute to Billy Joe Shaver (Live) *(2003),* Greatest Hits *(2006), and the* Live at Billy Bob's *CD and DVD (2012). In 2005, Woodall started the high-energy band, Jeremy Lynn Woodall & The Grinders, and in 2009 they released their debut album,* One Horse Town. *In 2019, Woodall paid tribute to Billy Joe Shaver on the album* Surrogate Son: A Tribute to Billy Joe Shaver, *which includes covers of fifteen Shaver-penned tunes.*

Adam Carter

Eddy Shaver is one of my three biggest influences as a guitarist. He was a phenomenal country music innovator. I heard *Tramp on Your Street* [at] around six years old, and my favorite song of Billy Joe's is "Tramp on Your Street." He talks about walking down the train tracks as a kid, going to see Hank Williams. He's hungry for it and trying to figure out his path. When I was four, I got to meet B. B. King, so I relate to it, and that record really got me looking at Eddy's guitar work. He was wild and ruthless onstage. It was cranked up guitar amps and loud as hell, like going to see The Who in 1970. Eddy was raunchy blues like Dickey Betts. Nashville didn't want that. They wanted clean Telecasters. Then, in the 2000s, you start seeing rock guitars coming into country music. He was doing that stuff twenty years before it was a thing. He played with his fingers and played slide in standard tuning instead of open tuning like a lot of guys do. [There were] all these little nuances that I've spent years listening to. Every time I listened to him again, there's something a little different that wasn't like last time. It was sad when he passed away. Nashville didn't know what they had.

Left to right: Billy Joe Shaver with a fourteen-year-old Adam Carter, Eddie's Attic, Decatur, Georgia, October 2008. Photo by Allyson Carter.

I ended up going to work [playing guitar] for Billy Joe for a couple years on and off as a teenager. My dad's in the military, so we traveled all over. I first met Billy Joe in 2008 at the White Elephant in Fort Worth, Texas. I was fourteen. My dad told Billy Joe how much of a fan he was, and how much of a fan I was of him and Eddy. He gave me an album he [had] just put out not long before. It was an old show from the nineties. Six months later, we went to see him play at Eddie's Attic in Decatur, Georgia, [near] where my dad's unit was stationed. At Eddie's Attic, you have to park in the back. So we park, get out, and it was like fate. This white Hummer pulls up, and Billy Joe gets out. We walk up and start talking to him. If you've ever met Billy, he's cool as a cucumber. Anybody can approach him in a parking lot, and he'll talk to them. He's as good as they come with fans. It's hard for the stadium acts to get to twenty thousand people, and Billy doesn't have that attendance, but shoot, he has to stand there after the show with three hundred people. That's a lot of people. He's easily out there forty-five minutes at the merch booth, talking to people, letting them get pictures and signing stuff.

He's as down-to-earth as any artist out there. Fifteen minutes into our conversation, he says, "Do you have your guitar with you?" "Yeah, why?" "You want to sit in with us?" He's never heard me play. That's Billy. That's how he is. It's all in the moment. I said, "Hell, yeah!" I was a fourteen-year-old getting to sit in with Billy Joe Shaver. That was cool. He gets me up and we do "Black Rose" and "You Asked Me To." At the end of the night, we swap phone numbers. He said he was going to hit me up. I didn't think about it. I thought he was just being nice. Six weeks later, my mom gets a phone call, and it was a guy named James that's friends with Billy. He was helping Billy manage some things at the time, doing his website, and that kind of thing. He says, "Billy wants you in Luckenbach, Texas, in a week for a video shoot that they're doing." It ended up being the *Live from Luckenbach* show that's out on DVD now. I didn't make the cut at that age, because I wasn't ready to be his road guy.

After that, we played a six-day run at the Exit/In in Nashville. Then he says, "It's not going to work out," and [he lets] me go. So, he goes off and [plays] two more shows. Then, he calls back and says, "Never mind. I got to have you. I'm telling you." I love the man to death, but he was back and forth constantly. I say, "Well, yeah, I'll do it." I'm a kid—it's not like I've got a work schedule—[and have] nothing to work around, so I'll just go and do whatever. The show was with Willie Nelson at a place like a truck stop he owned called Willie's Place in Carl's Corner, Texas. That was the first time I ever got to play with Willie Nelson. It was badass. Being a kid and being able to do all that stuff was awesome. From that point forward, it was a six-month stretch, eight-month stretch, and then he took a break for a year and didn't play at all. Then, when he came back from that period, it's around 2012, and I've probably done ten dates with him since.

Billy Joe's great at cues, very up-front. He'll tell you if he doesn't like something, which is good if you're a sideman. He'll make you work. He's not always the best at telling you and getting it across, but he knows what he wants and doesn't mind telling you, but you might have to decipher, because he's not a "guitar player." He just plays enough to write. So it's fun working with him, because there's room for your own interpretation. He's not saying exactly what he wants, he's willing to let you communicate in the same vein.

Billy Joe is literally a honky-tonk hero. He grew up in a bar watching drugs, drinking, and fighting, and when he writes about it, it's real. He knows all that lingo and oozes that vibe. What he says, anybody can understand. It's just his choice of words. All the great songwriters I've ever met in my life always told me that a good songwriter can write something down and tell you something in ten words, but a great songwriter can take those same ten words and tell you the same exact thing in five. And that's Billy's thing, because he's got a great vocabulary. There's not a lot of guys out there like that. Billy Joe's the last of his generation, with the Stones and the Beatles. Nowadays with popular music, it feels like there's no time spent on songwriting. That blood, sweat, and tears of learning different things and focusing and trying to do better is gone. Lost. Now a lot of it is shallow. Billy, Willie, Waylon, guys like that, used to sit and play all day long. They might go on a binge and sit there for a week and not even leave, just sit with the guitars and write. You don't see that a lot these days because of how the business works. People used to have writing retreats, just friends getting together. You don't hear about it much [any] more. It was, "Hey, man, can you meet me down here on Seventeenth Avenue from ten to one, and we're going to write for three hours. If we don't come up with something, whatever." They didn't write on command. They wrote on emotion.

Billy Joe does an emotional a capella version of "Star in My Heart" at every show. He wrote the song for Eddy, and it's on the last album that Eddy was ever on, called *The Earth Rolls On*. He does it by himself, and it chokes him up a little to think to have to sing it. He lost his mom and his ex-wife Brenda. They stayed very close up until she died even though they weren't married. Then they lost Eddy. If lost my son, I don't know what I would do, and it was all within a year or two of each other. It took a toll on him. Billy Joe and I are still friends and talk regularly. He's a good guy. He helped me get in this business. I always loved playing music, but I never considered it something I could do for a living. He showed me I could. It worked out. I thank God we crossed paths. I'm forever indebted to him.[9]

Adam Carter, born April 22, 1994, in Westminster, South Carolina, started playing classic blues and rock guitar at age seven. Carter, who counts Eddy Shaver as one of his three greatest influences, landed a gig touring with Billy Joe Shaver at age fifteen. He has also shared stages with fellow country artists Brad Paisley, Willie Nelson, Ray Price, and Loretta Lynn.

Brian Whelan

Ray Kennedy called me to play a five-show run in Southern California with Billy Joe Shaver, but I was still working for Dwight Yoakam and had a conflict on one of the nights, so I couldn't play any of them. I went and saw Billy Joe at Spaceland [in Los Angeles]. I didn't get to meet him. I'm not sure if I'd want to. The guy who did guitar that night got chewed out onstage, on the mic, by Billy Joe. There's part of me that wishes I did do the gig. Maybe he would have liked me. Then there's another part of me that thought, *Would he like anybody?*

There are so many bands like Journey, where you see them, and their show is all planned out. They play casinos, working these circuits where it's professional and the same every time. There's no sense of it potentially falling apart and going off the rails. There's very little of it nowadays because if you fuck up your live shows, you're fucked. People won't buy your records. Even bands like Blackberry Smoke. They start on time, they're nice to the promoter, they don't break up the greenroom. Billy Joe is unpredictable. It could fall apart anytime like Jerry Lee Lewis and the Sex Pistols. He's the bridge between that. It comes from that rock and roll chaos mentality. The show that I saw was untethered. Most people don't do it. They care too much about being professional and tight.

He did what Chuck Berry did, have a band of people he's never met show up, and, with no rehearsal, they're supposed to know the songs. He doesn't even play guitar, and the band's flying by the seat of their pants. He was starting and stopping songs randomly and would berate the guitar player. He did this drum solo bit where he goes backstage in the middle of the show, and the drummer plays a solo for ten minutes. I remember he was drinking a lot of Red Bull. He was drinking the shit out of them. I don't think he was enjoying the show. I don't know him enough to know, but a lot of people from Texas and Appalachia come

Brian Whelan. Photo by Micah Albert.

play in Los Angeles, and they just don't have fun. If you play for rowdy Texas dancehall crowds and you go to Los Angeles, it's way different. The audiences are cold. That's the vibe. This type of music requires give and take with the audience. When you don't get it, that's the danger. You go through the motions, but this show had a wild energy.

The first time I heard Billy Joe's music was when I was with was with my first band here in Los Angeles, called [the] Smooth Pursuit. I was around twenty years old, and it was the first rock band I had where there were elements of American roots music, which is the path I went on. The guitar player was a Texan from Amarillo. He was older than me and played a lot of Texas music that I was hearing for the first time. One of the things that I liked the best was *Tramp on Your Street*, particularly the title track and the remake of "I Been to Georgia on a Fast Train." That song's an amazing performance by Eddy on guitar, a great song across the board. I love a song that's good and catchy. That song's a country standard now, and it's 100 percent true. He's not playing a character or using symbolism. When a song can be relatable and heard all over the world, and it's just a guy singing about himself and life, it's [special].

I'm a big fan of Billy Joe, but I'm a bigger fan of Eddy. He's a huge influence on my guitar playing. I first heard him when he was playing for Todd Snider. I was a fan of Todd from an early age, and Eddy was the lead guitar player on his first record [*Songs for the Daily Planet*]. If you put *Songs for the Daily Planet* and *Tramp on Your Street* together, Eddy had a very distinct sound. It was more Chuck Berry than country. Chuck Berry is one of my favorite guitar players, and the guitar players I like are all doing their best version of Chuck Berry. Guys like Keith Richards and Eddy were doing that. It spoke to me. Whenever anyone's influenced by that, I gravitate towards it before I can even explain why. Eddy was a sub for [guitar player] Pete Anderson in [Dwight's band] in the early days. Pete would want to produce and stay in Los Angeles. So that's how Eddy wound up playing for Dwight, and Dwight always had great things to say about Eddy. He told me a great story about him. Dwight was making him play a Fender Deluxe amp, and Eddy stored his Marshall under the stage, and no one could figure out why it was so loud—[it was] because Eddy and his guitar tech conspired and hid the Marshall under the stage.

The thing that's so influential about Billy Joe Shaver is his willing-ness to be real. What a lot of people look for in songs is authenticity, the feeling that the person they are listening to is real. Billy Joe Shaver has that in spades. He channels his experiences and turns it into great music. He writes songs that are catchy, hooky, relatable, and completely true. Putting your own life into a song where it interests someone else is very hard to do. That transparency is his influence on me. There are not many people who write with such clarity. Radiohead are shrouded in psychedelic language. Billy Joe is not. He writes about his experience and thoughts in stark, literal terms, and he was the craziest guy in the outlaw movement. He was the closest to the edge. When you say that about a group that includes Steve Earle and Townes Van Zandt? That's far out. Billy Joe's the real deal. The genuine article.[10]

Brian Whelan, born January 22, 1982, in Seattle, is a Los Angeles–based singer-songwriter, musician, and record producer. In 2012, Whelan released his debut solo album, The Decider. *For years, he was a key member of Dwight Yoakam's band, which he departed in 2015. His 2016 release,* Sugarland, *kicks off with the track "Americana," a satirical commentary on the labeling of the genre.*

Jason McKenzie

I hadn't really heard of Billy Joe Shaver until I started playing with him. I studied jazz at the University of North Texas in Denton, and, when I moved to Austin in 1997, I played in a jazz big band for fun. A bass player from Sweden named Hans was playing with Billy Joe and got me the gig as his drummer. That's when I started to realize how much influence Billy Joe had on the outlaw country movement. He was growing a beard and wearing denim jackets and jeans when everybody else was in bolos and blazers, and his lyrics were raw. He uses deceptively simple language to tap into deep truths.

We got mixed reviews in the nineties. Some people seemed to liked it, some didn't. I always liked it when we played to crowds where everyone was standing up against the stage like a rock show. Then we'd play places where it's an older crowd, and they're sitting at little round tables. Eddy was super loud and turned his amp backwards and put a blanket over it. When the show started, he would test his guitar, and it'd be super loud. Billy just kind of went with it. He'd get on the mic and say, "We're fixin' to peel some paint." One person described it as "The singer doesn't

Left to right: Jeremy Lynn Woodall on guitar, Jason McKenzie on drums, and Billy Joe Shaver at the microphone, City Winery, Nashville, Tennessee. Photo by Kathy Reid-Papson.

know he's in a rock band, and the guitar player doesn't know he's in a country band." Hans was a little bit of a cheesy guy and called it heavy metal honky-tonk.

Billy Joe had me play drum solos, and he'd walk off. The first time it happened I was in Belgium in front of a huge crowd. It was a Legends of Rock and Roll concert with B. B. King, Little Richard, and Chuck Berry. They put us on the bill last minute. We took Carl Perkins's place because he was sick. Eddy broke a string, and they both look at me like, "Just do something." So I did a drum solo in front of five thousand people. Billy Joe loved it, so he started incorporating it in the show, even though I never asked for it. I wouldn't think the country crowd would like a drum solo, but I figured out how to do a solo that enabled me to do the same things every night, but something different too. As a drummer, I always loved playing with him because he never told me how to play unless I was doing something like a drum fill that was stepping over his words. He let me play how I wanted, and he even liked it if I changed up how I played songs instead of playing them the same year after year.

Eddy liked having a tough persona. He liked to play guitar with a cigarette dangling from his lips. He sometimes had an attitude with people who didn't know him, but he was a nice guy underneath it all. He liked to talk about music and was really into buying magazines. Everywhere we went, he'd buy *Maxim* magazines and look at the women. Not the nudie mags. He just liked looking at models. His relationship with Billy Joe was kind of strange. They would fight a lot. They were more like brothers than father and son.

I quit the band not long before Eddy passed, but we were still in touch, and I was on his radar. He wanted me to play on his solo record in Dallas. I made a trip of it. He was supposed to be in there a few days later, but I guess he decided to visit some old friends [in Waco] and enjoy a New Year's Eve party. He died that night. I found out the next day, calling the producer. It was weird. Billy Joe had a gig that night at Poodies outside of Austin, and he did it anyway to keep from going crazy. Willie Nelson showed up. It was touching.

Billy Joe's a great and generous bandleader. If we weren't playing a lot, he'd pay us double for a festival to make it up. At the end of a tour, he'd give us an extra hundred or two. He also liked gambling, so anytime we were in Oklahoma or Louisiana, he'd give you a hundred bucks to gamble with. I was a shitty gambler. I didn't go to the roulette table; I'd play the penny slots and pocket the money. He could also be volatile. He fired me and a guitar player several times, but he has a strong moral code about money. He would always give us severance pay and then end up hiring us back.

[We were on the road one time and] didn't have any gigs in Los Angeles, but we decided to stop at the Santa Monica Pier. When we went into the restaurant, they were being snooty to him, and I was just thinking, *We should just go somewhere else.* Then the manager recognized him from being in the movie *The Apostle*, sat us by a window, gave us champagne and the four-star treatment. But Billy Joe's favorite is Waffle House. I always had to find one on Google or Yelp. His idea of pampering himself was Cracker Barrel.

I think Billy's on the spectrum of being a little bit bipolar. I've seen it when he gets angry. He changes into a different person. He gets into a mode where he cannot hear what you're saying. He's done that with me a couple times. You'll try to say, "No. Billy, I didn't mean it that way." He can't hear you. He would get really mad at me if I started asking like, "Hey, are we going to be touring in two months from now because I have this other project I'm doing here." He did not want to hear about other projects. Man. He would get so mad. He would think that I was plotting to leave. In his defense, I left in 1999, and came back for South by Southwest in 2007. If you had a troubled childhood it can bring it out, and I think he had some abandonment issues from when he was a kid that made him less trustful of people. He would get paranoid. He'd talk about the old days in Nashville. He thought Minnie Pearl from *Hee Haw* was a devil worshiper. He didn't like Glen Campbell because of the way he treated Tanya Tucker. They almost got into a fight at a party.

I recently dated a girl with [bipolar disorder] and she called it her "superpower." There's clairvoyance that comes with it that can't be explained. I've seen some weird, strange phenomena around Billy Joe. We were in San Diego eating breakfast at this place on the beach, and he says, "Somebody should close that window, or a bird will fly in here." We thought, *What? That's absurd.* All of a sudden, a bird flew in.

I was in Taiwan at the airport with my other band when the shooting happened. CNN was on and they announce, "Country songwriter Billy Joe Shaver arrested for shooting someone." I was, like, *What?* [Shortly after], I wound up back on tour with him. At that time, the bass player was Nick Gaitan. He had a rockabilly feel on the upright. What I liked about him was that I could play a smaller vintage kit for acoustic stuff. We would do a miniature acoustic set that would kick off the night with "Live Forever" and then go into "Bottom Dollar." I'd use brushes. I thought it sounded really good. So Nick was really into 1950s and 1960s blues. I was into jazz and 1970s rock. I had a Led Zeppelin feel. Jeremy Woodall came out of the 1980s like Motley Crue. He had a Slash vibe mixed with country. We had all the decades covered.

Billy Joe is just amazing. His storytelling and wit. He just goes with the flow. If the guitar player is suddenly having trouble with a pedal, he'll [distract] the attention and engage the audience. If someone tries to heckle, he's so quick with the comeback he puts them to shame and makes everyone laugh. He didn't like to talk about the shooting, because the trial hadn't come up, but one time someone said, "Billy, can you tell us about the shooting?" He stared out for a second. I thought, *Uh-oh. What's he going to say?* He made a joke out of it. He says, "Oh my god! When's it going to happen?" But he doesn't remember saying "Where do you want it?" He thinks maybe he said, "Why do you want this?" and it was misheard through the grapevine. It makes sense. I can hear him saying, "Why do you want this?" But I honestly don't know.[11]

Jason McKenzie, born April 8, 1970 in Tallahassee, Florida, is a professional drummer who began studying drums under Butch Trucks from the Allman Brothers at age fifteen. He studied symphonic percussion at Florida State and then transferred to the University of North Texas to focus on jazz. After college, he moved to Austin and studied with tabla teacher Aloke Dutta, and he went to India twice to study tabla. McKenzie played drums with Shaver for nearly a decade, beginning in the nineties, and appeared on The Late Show with David Letterman *with Shaver and Willie Nelson in 2014. He is a member of Austin-based world music ambassadors Atash.*

Wacko from Waco

"Where do you want it?" Billy Joe Shaver allegedly asked Billy Bryant Coker on March 31, 2007, seconds before shooting him in the face outside Papa Joe's Saloon, a neighborhood bar in Lorena, Texas, south of Waco where Shaver was living at the time.[1] Shaver, who had not been to Papa Joe's prior to that evening, had stopped off for a beer with his second wife, Wanda, after spending the day taking pictures of graveyard angels for his 2007 spiritual album, *Everybody's Brother*.

Coker instigated the dispute. He approached Shaver inside the bar and claimed he knew him. Coker then grabbed Shaver by the shoulders and said sternly, "You sit over here." He took out a long, serrated flip-blade and stirred Shaver and Wanda's beers with the knife.[2] Coker was approximately fifty at the time and had an intimidating stature in comparison to seventy year old Shaver, who just a few years before had suffered a heart attack onstage during a performance at Gruene Hall in New Braunfels, Texas. (In the midst of the heart attack, Shaver had fallen to his knees, popped what was thought to be a nitroglycerin tablet, gotten up, and finished the gig before seeking medical attention.)[3]

At Papa Joe's, Shaver tried desperately to end the situation as it escalated. He put his hand on his wife's shoulder and said, "Wanda, we need to leave." Coker turned around with his knife in his hand and said, "Why don't you just shut the fuck up?"[4] Shaver told Coker that everything could be settled with an apology. Coker disagreed. He said he was going to kill Shaver and headed for the back door to take the fight outside. Shaver got out of the bar first, and Coker followed close behind.

Billy Joe Shaver performs at Waterloo Records after posting bond, Austin, Texas, April 3, 2007. Photo by Brian T. Atkinson.

Fearing for his life, Shaver grabbed his .22 derringer from his car. He was permitted to carry the handgun as a deputy sheriff in Waco.[5] Outside, Coker made a jabbing motion, insinuating he was going to stab Shaver, who was under the impression that Coker also had a gun.

According to the original police affidavit, Shaver is said to have asked Coker before he drew his weapon, "Where do you want it?" or, as Shaver contended, "Why do you want this?"[6] Coker didn't answer. Shaver settled on his face. He pulled the .22 from his left pocket, aimed it at Coker, and said "Mother," pulled the trigger, then "fucker." "I shot him," Shaver said, "right between the 'mother' and the 'fucker.'"[7] The bullet hit Coker in the jaw and lodged in his neck. The injury wasn't fatal. "It was," Shaver said, "a lucky shot."[8]

Shaver hid out in a motel in Waco that evening but turned himself in at McLennan County Jail in Waco on April 3, 2007, following a warrant issued in his name. He was released in an hour after paying a $50,000 bond.[9] He played his scheduled gig that afternoon at Waterloo Records in Austin. "Shaver was running about 45 minutes late," says Brian T. Atkinson who was there that afternoon. "The room was packed and electric with anticipation. We all knew why he was late and wondered if he'd make it from jail to Waterloo at all. He rolled in almost an hour after start time and put on a perfect show like nothing at all had happened."[10]

It was not until April 2010 that Shaver stood trial at the McLennan County Courthouse, facing a twenty-year sentence on aggravated assault charges.[11] The trial was a spectacle, with Shaver's longtime friends Willie Nelson and Robert Duvall seated in the first two rows.[12] Shaver had met Duvall while the actor was filming the 1988 Emmy-winning miniseries *Lonesome Dove*, an adaptation of the 1985 novel written by Texas native Larry McMurtry. (Duvall also appeared in Shaver's 2002 music video for the title track of his album *Freedom's Child*.) Seated behind Duvall was Willie Nelson, who took the stand as a character witness.

The court case did not seem to be in Shaver's favor, but he knew in his heart he would walk out a free man, continuing to book gigs for dates after the trial. Following a successful self-defense plea, Shaver was acquitted on April 9, 2010. The jury deliberated for less than two hours.[13] Outside the courtroom Shaver said, "I am very sorry about the incident. Hopefully things will work out where we become friends enough so that he gives me back my bullet."[14] Then Shaver drove three hours to Houston to play a scheduled gig at the Firehouse Saloon. "I got in some trouble here awhile back and just got out of it today," Shaver said onstage. "And praise the Lord my God, praise the God. My God. Praise the Lord is right. Praise the Lord and thank you, thank you so much for your prayers and stuff. You people that were putting curses and things on people, you can lift 'em now, and the voodoo dolls, sell 'em for five bucks apiece."

"I own three of 'em," replied Shaver's longtime friend Dale Watson ("I Lie When I Drink"), who was onstage with him at the time.[15] When Watson heard the news of Shaver's acquittal earlier that evening, he was going to call Shaver but realized they were then both performing in Houston. So, as soon as Watson finished his show, he drove across town to the Firehouse Saloon to congratulate Billy Joe.[16] Watson performed the song, "Where Do You Want It?" which he wrote in 2007 and is on his album *El Rancho Azul* (2013). The song, based on the shooting, was first recorded by Whitey Morgan and the 78's on their eponymous 2010 sophomore album. During the trial, Watson's song was brought up by the prosecution and used against Shaver.[17] Shaver himself didn't write a song about the incident until years later with his Willie Nelson cowrite and musical interpretation of the events, "Wacko from Waco," which appears on his album *Live at Billy Bob's Texas* (2012).

Dale Watson

"Where Do You Want It?" was just a total made-up song. I wrote it onstage at Chicken Shit Bingo [at Ginny's Little Longhorn in Austin]. I had heard about Billy Joe shooting Billy Coker in the face, just like everybody else [had], from newspapers and TV. It was how I thought the shooting would have gone down. I called Billy a couple days after, because I just wrote the song off the cuff. I said, "I just made it up onstage. I'd rather get the story from you." "Well, Dale, I can't really say anything about it. I can't say anything about what happened." "I'll throw the song away if you want me to." "No, no, no. A song's like your babies. You do what you want with that song, keep doing it." I had no idea it would affect his trial. I was just going by hearsay, what was said on the news. That's the bad thing about stuff like that. People get tried before they go on trial just by hearsay. I wrote it as an admiration of Billy. It takes a lot to

Dale Watson (*at microphone*), Ameripolitan Awards weekend, Memphis, Tennessee, February 24, 2019. Photo by Mark Whitfield Lennon.

provoke him, to rile him up. He's one of the nicest guys in the world. He's the kind outlaw. It really worried me that he could have gone to jail over my dumb song. I just love the guy, from the talent he has to who he is.

I was aware of Billy Joe Shaver's songwriting from day one. My dad was a picker, and every Sunday he'd play an album on his record player, take his guitar and amp, and play along with it. Waylon Jennings's *Honky Tonk Heroes* is one of them albums. That's where I learned about Billy Joe's writing. He wrote every song except "We Had It All" [written by Troy Seals and Donnie Frits]. The lyrics strike me the most about his songwriting. He has a way, very much like Merle Haggard, but more of a honk-tonk Merle Haggard. You can tell that Merle is the poor man's poet. Billy's a cotton picker in the way he writes. He was a guy who got his hands dirty and would go to a place like Papa Joe's and have a beer just like a regular guy. Not that Merle wasn't, but he got success and was able to get out of the life. Billy Joe had a lot of success as a songwriter, but he always had some sort of anonymity that Merle couldn't have. I think his writing is reflected in that. He's just a Joe Six-Pack.

I met him for the first time at a festival in 1994. Our mutual friend Willie Nelson was there. I think we might have met on Willie's bus. It was somewhere in the Willie sphere. Billy Joe had heard of me, and he asked, "You live in Austin, don't you?" "Yeah. You're a hero of mine." I thought he had a house in Nashville. "No. I'm back in Waco. I hate Nashville." So we had a common ground right away.

I'd run into him constantly over the years because he's a road dog like me. We'd try to go see him, and he'd pop in on some of our gigs. When they started filming a documentary on him called *A Portrait of Billy Joe* [directed by Luciana Pedraza, released in 2004], and he had a camera crew following him around, he called and asked me "Where do I take these people? They're all up my ass. I've lost places to take them. Can I come over to Chicken Shit Bingo and sit in with you?"

We were gonna try to accommodate the camera crew, but Billy wouldn't have any part. He said, "I don't want any special treatment." They wanted to get pictures of him in front of the line getting his ticket. He didn't want to be at the front of the line. He was number five or six and asked everyone he went ahead of "Are you okay with this?" He's always very thoughtful. Not pulling the I'm-the-star card. He did that, and he came in. The chicken shit on a number within ten minutes of getting there, and within another five minutes it shit on Billy's number. We didn't rig it. You can't rig chicken shit. When he got called to take his winnings, he put it in our tip jar, sang a song, and said good-bye. He was shining in a way that he always does the whole time by being thoughtful and thinking of everyone else first. It always impresses me.

I gave Billy Joe the Ameripolitan Founder of the Sound Award in 2015 because I wanted to give him the recognition he deserved. I started the Ameripolitan genre in 2014 because I thought, *We're getting wet. We're getting no love over here. We're getting ignored like an old violin that don't work no more.* Outlaw country, western swing, rockabilly, honky-tonk [weren't] represented by any genre. All that music is constantly ignored by the mainstream. They think it's oldies, and it ain't. Billy's music sounds like classics, and the songs should be classics. Billy's the guy that if you want to write an outlaw song, he'd teach you.

It's important to keep his music alive for future generations because nobody writes like him. It's as important to have his music preserved as it is Hank Williams's. Billy does not get enough credit. It's crazy. He never played the game. His songs mostly got recorded when all the game was getting a song to the artist. Billy Joe is like a college professor.

What he does and how he does it is a lost trade, and it needs to be there to let people know how to write a damn song. My favorite song of his is probably "Live Forever." It's got a spiritual tone to it like Billy always has, a songwriter's lament, a song that every good ole boy can identify with.[18]

Dale Watson, born October 7, 1962, in Birmingham, Alabama, is the Austin- and Memphis-based founder of the Ameripolitan genre. Watson began writing songs at age twelve and started a performing career by playing the Houston club circuit. He moved to Los Angeles in the late eighties on the advice of friend Rosie Flores and played in the house band at the famous Palomino Club in North Hollywood. After relocating to Austin, Watson scored a deal with Hightone Records and released his landmark honky-tonk debut, Cheatin' Heart Attack. *Watson teamed up with western swing legend and Asleep at the Wheel front man Ray Benson on the 2016 album* Dale and Ray, *which included the song "Feelin' Haggard," a tribute to the late Merle Haggard. Watson says he writes most of his songs onstage or while driving his tour bus.*

Nick Gaitan

It's a funny story how I became Billy Joe Shaver's bass player. I was living in Houston, and Brad Turcotte from Compadre Records called me up to play bass for a local artist. At the time, Billy Joe was on Compadre, but it had nothing to do with him. I showed up, and the girl was kind of country. I said, "You ought to ask them to let me play the upright bass on this song." My electric chops at the time weren't there for country. She said, "Oh, damn, you play that? Cool." I showed her my upright bass skills. The song was a slow country piece, and we nailed it. After that, we shook hands, and everybody went home. I didn't hear from anyone after that. She went on and did her thing, and I kept doing my business around Houston. I swear, at the time, I was working the entire block of 3700 Main Street, which is where our Continental Club is. I was bartending, selling records in a record shop, and teaching [music] down the street at Houston Community College.

Six months later, I was on my way home from a shitty Monday night gig somewhere and checked my messages. Out of nowhere, there's one

Nick Gaitan (back) with Billy Joe Shaver.

Right to left: Nick Gaitan, Billy Joe Shaver, Jason McKenzie, and Jeremy Lynn Woodall stop at a Waffle House on tour. Photo courtesy of Nick Gaitan.

from Brad Turcotte. He says, "Hey, this is Brad. I met you a while back. I have a job for you. I want you to be Billy Joe Shaver's bass player." I got him on the phone, and we talked out the details. Then I went to visit him at his office at Music World Entertainment. We made our deal, and I was hired. I quit five jobs, and it was just a matter of time until I showed up in Waco.

I had to learn his songs from a live CD recorded in London. The guys backing him were Diamondback TX. While I'm learning them, I'm getting hit by the intensity. By the time "Star in My Heart" comes on, I'm in my head so deep, it was a rollercoaster of emotion. It was a big deal for me. Then I took a break. I thought, Let's see what Billy Joe Shaver is up to lately. I Google "Billy Joe Shaver," click "news," and the search engine pulls up hundreds of pictures of him in an orange jumpsuit. I thought, *What the fuck? He just shot somebody? Oh, man. I just quit all my jobs. How long is this is going to last? When's his trial? Son of a bitch, what's going to happen now?*

I didn't have a car. I did everything by foot, bike, or bus. I hadn't ever played with a touring band before. I figured somebody was going to pick me up and take me to Waco. I asked Brad, "What do y'all do when people in his band need to get there?" "Nick, the old man is my problem, and that's my only problem. You have to figure out how you're going to do this." "Am I supposed to meet him at a Flying J or one of those local truck stops?" "No, you just go to his door and knock." "Shit, okay."

I called up my sister, and she said, "No, dude, you ain't going to miss this opportunity. I'm taking you tonight. Let's go." So [she] and her friend took me to Waco in a pickup truck that night. The next morning, I pull up to Billy Joe's and it's drizzling. I'm at the back of the truck trying to wrap my gear with large trash bags because everything's getting wet. Finally, I knock on his door, and there he is. He's got two pit bulls that wanted to kick the door down. He pulls them back, looks at me, and says, "You're the guy from Houston?" "Yes, sir." "All right. Hold on a second." He puts the dogs up, comes back, and invites me in. We have a little bit of small talk, and the next thing you know, the bus pulls up, and Billy Joe is going back and forth grabbing things. Grabbing all his blue denim shirts. He says, "Did you learn all my songs?" I said, "Yeah." "You feel good about them?" "I do. I'll do my best." "I know you will."

We had a whole lot to bond about because we spent a lot of time on the bus or in the van together. He always treated me well and was cool to me. I can't tell you what he thinks of me, but he always treated me like a real friend. We'd laugh a lot and tell stories, but mostly I'd listen to him because I was learning so much being around him. As his upright bass player, I could tell that he loves the blues, because a lot of his stuff was blues. So we would talk about songs and what we appreciated. We talked a lot about Willie Dixon [the bluesman best known for "Hoochie Coochie Man"]. I told him how much I liked Willie Dixon. He said, "Oh man. He's the best." Then he'd go into talking about Muddy Waters and a lot of those badass Chess Records guys. We bonded over a lot of cool stuff. If it wasn't music, it was old stories and poetry.

Billy Joe had a lot of people coming in and out of his band. The group he had rolling from the time I joined were about five guys that were between managers and drivers. When everything was greased and we were rolling, it was me, Billy Joe, Jeremy Lynn Woodall, and Jason McKenzie. That's the lineup I spent the most time with. That group was a well-oiled machine. We could just adjust with him. Anything that would happen onstage evened out. It was the perfect combination.

Playing in in his band was a wide spectrum of things. First and foremost, it was amazing and a huge deal for me because he's a heavyweight who's influenced just about everything you've heard. I loved being in his band. It could be glorious, but it could be stressful at times. We were always rushing to get somewhere because we didn't leave Waco on time. In 2009, we played the Hardly Strictly Bluegrass Festival. It was a big festival with a huge lineup, but we had a subpar guitar player because a few nights earlier [Billy Joe] had a falling out with Jeremy. He was only out a few weeks. It was weird, but everything went beautifully. We kicked ass. That festival really stays with me because not only was I with one of my heroes, but I also got to meet Richie Havens, Dave Alvin, and Guy Clark. The day after we played, we were flying out to Kansas City for Farm Aid. We missed the flight. Shit would always happen, but this time we were waiting around for the flight, trying to find a seat at the airport gate, and there's Guy Clark just sitting there. I can hear Billy now, "Hey, Guy!" These two cats are talking, and finally we fly out of San Francisco and get to Farm Aid. Well, our slot was already done so we didn't get to play Billy's music, but we got to meet Willie on his bus. There's Lukas

Nelson, Jamey Johnson, and a few other people. We're all hanging out, having a good time, and Willie says, "Why don't y'all come up onstage with me?" He brought everyone up at the end for a big group version of "Will the Circle Be Unbroken." So we did get on the Farm Aid stage that year with Willie. All this stuff happened in twenty-four hours. I'll never forget it.

When the trial came, we weren't sure if he was going to get acquitted. I thought, *This has got to be a lot of trouble because it has to do with a gun and a bar, which you're never legally able to mix.* So I was worried. I said, "If he gets taken to jail, this is not going to be good." I didn't know what to feel. I was in the courtroom playing real close attention to see what was really going on and, of course, getting a kick out of everybody else getting a kick out of it. It was wild. There were people jumping and screaming. When the prosecutor would try to nail him and say something slick, Billy Joe would talk back. She was suggesting that he started shit intentionally. "You just got into a fight to brag about it in a song later, or you'll just write a book about it." Billy Joe says, "Lady, I wish they'd write a book about you." He'd cause uproars of laughter. I remember this guy jumps up and says, "Come on, woman!" When Willie walked into the court-room, everybody freaked out because they said he was a witness. He wasn't there when the shooting happened, but he was a witness because Billy called him right after [the shooting]. Robert Duvall was there too. Tons of supporters. It was a real trip to see the witnesses who all came from different places. There was one guy who had been sitting in the parking lot of Papa Joe's in his van rolling a joint or something. He heard the bang, but he didn't see a gun. Coker's character took some punches because people were telling it straight. Even the bar owner said, "I think he's arrogant." So they were slamming him. Watching Dick DeGuerin go to work as Billy's defense attorney was amazing. He said to Coker, "I bet you won't go stirring people's drinks with knives anymore, now will you?"

The trial was nuts, a trip. Billy Joe ends up getting acquitted on a Friday. Walking down the steps from the courthouse, there's news cameras, and they're saying, "Mr. Shaver, how do you feel that you've just been acquitted?" He says, "I feel great." "Do you have a message for the Coker family?" I'm in an earshot, and he says, "Well, yeah. I'm really sorry all this happened, and I hope we can become good enough friends [that] I can get my bullet back." The faces on the people were amazing. The camera guy looks around like, "What did he just say?" We're all cracking up. Somebody snapped a shot, and we're all thrown back in laughter, and Billy and Dick are both smiling. Then they ask, "What are you going to do to celebrate?" He says, "I'm going to go down to Houston [to] play a show."

Right around six p.m., we're finally to ourselves, and Billy says, "Nick, I'm going to go pick up the car. The Mercedes. Can you drive Lightning to Houston?" He tosses me the keys, "Yeah. I got it." I jump in the van right onto Highway 6 and got a head start for Houston because we had to load in at nine p.m. I didn't hit much traffic. The drive was boring, but it was significant and symbolic because of what [had] just happened in real life. We were all excited that our friend wasn't going to jail, and we didn't have to be worried about it or stress anymore. We lit up the show, like we always do, that night and made an announcement that he was acquitted. We're just so happy. Even Dale Watson popped in. He knew that Billy was there and goes up and plays "You Asked Me To." He also did "Where Do You Want It?" But Billy Joe stands behind the fact that he did not say "Where do you want it?"

After [I had been] in the band for about four years, he let me go. Then I got a call from him in October 2014 asking me if I wanted to play with him again. I said, "Hell, yeah, I do!" So I got back in his band the second time, and some of the first gigs were with Willie out in Helotes, Texas, at Floore's Country Store. December of that year, we played the *Late Show with David Letterman* with Willie. When I found out we were going to be on, I thought, *This is so cool.* I didn't tell many people because I didn't want to jinx it. We drove up to New York for it in Billy's Sprinter van just like any other gig. We're out in the hotel, [in] Hudson Yards, and we get a call from John Selman in Willie's crew. He says, "Hey, we need you guys to load in." So we hurried and show up around nine a.m. You're at the Ed Sullivan Theater where all your rock and roll heroes played, and you're with these amazing singer-songwriters who are stars. It was a big deal for me and for friends and family back home, but it was just a day's work when you put everything into context. It's no different than playing a neighborhood bar. We did some rehearsals, played, and then we went off to another gig at the City Winery in New York. We finished the gig early and headed back to the hotel. It was raining, so I couldn't go out and celebrate. I decided I was going to watch the show, so I ordered some food and stayed at the hotel, but by the time I got settled in, I missed the episode by about ten minutes.

I thought I'd traveled a lot before Billy Joe, and that'd I'd done big things, but I learned that I hadn't. Being in his band kicked it into gear. I learned that he really does care about other people. He always took care of his band. He's a genuine and generous bandleader. There was never a situation where I was left out or had to do without. You just got to take care of Billy and he'll take care of the band. That's the experience I had. He was always generous and giving to people. I've seen him give strangers $100 out of nowhere. I remember being at a gas station on a break. I'd have stuff on the counter, and he'd say, "Hey, I got that." I'd say, "Man that's okay." "Don't worry about it. It's just money. It'll go away." So there were lessons in generosity and selflessness with him. That was his attitude. It was amazing just being around him.

I learned about the specifics of the business. I learned about songwriting just by being in his presence. The process of paying attention to the way he handles things and what inspires him. "This is how it works." You're watching a master of [his] craft. He'd throw words out about a lonely beer bottle sitting in a puddle, just singing to himself. He'd do that, and you'd see the wheels turning. There's a huge unbeatable strength and vulnerability to Billy Joe. You think, *Oh, my god, where did he come up with this? How did you paint that feeling into a picture with words?* His writing is from a completely honest place. There's no mistaking it. There's only one version of the truth, and that's his strength as a songwriter.

Billy Joe's never tried to be anybody other than Billy Joe. His words are how his heart feels. In one hundred years from now, I think there's going to be even more reasons people should know about this great songwriter. He's already important to so many people. Even if you look around at the cast of characters in the outlaw movement, the people who covered his songs, and who he influenced, he holds great importance. He's the high-water mark. That's going to be his legacy. We're going to look back and say, let's trace this song down, and so many things will go right back to Billy Joe Shaver. It's the same way when you listen to rock and roll and the blues. Somebody who is a fan of Led Zeppelin can go back to Willie Dixon. It all goes back to one significant person, and [with progressive country] that's Billy Joe. *Honky Tonk Heroes* says it all. It's heavy, but it didn't stop with Waylon doing those songs. There's so many people who were influenced by it. Billy Joe kicked fire into the outlaw movement. It's that simple. It's influence beyond genre. His writing transcends, and his legacy will carry on.[19]

Nick Gaitan is a native of Houston and grew up in the working-class area of the city on the sounds of Tejano, rock and roll, country, and soul that influenced him from a young age. Gaitan became Billy Joe Shaver's bass player in 2007 and toured with him on and off for a decade. His band The Umbrella Man recorded their self-titled debut in 2009 and released the album Bridges and Bayous *in 2012. He has also toured with rock and roll singer Nikki Hill.*

Brian Wright

Billy Joe Shaver is the real outlaw who lived down the street from me as a kid and [when I was] a teenager living with other musicians. We knew who he was, and he'd walk his dogs by our house all the time, but we were scared to bother him and didn't want to go up to or talk to him. He's unsung to the population at large with status in Waco. When I learned he wrote "Honky Tonk Heroes" and dug deeper, I realized the greatness of this unknown songwriter from our town looking for redemption in his songs with self-deprecating humor, ranked up there with Townes Van Zandt and Guy Clark

When the shooting happened, I was living in Austin, and my dad called me, "You hear what old Billy Joe Shaver did?" We weren't surprised. It wasn't Billy Joe [causing trouble]. I grew up a mile away from Papa Joe's. It's a little honky-tonk bar that looks like a shed on the outside in a part of town with some pretty country folks who aren't afraid to shoot someone. A few years later, I opened for Billy Joe at Eddie's Attic [near] Atlanta. Standing at the merch table afterwards, a fan brought him a taser and said, "Here, man. This way you don't got to shoot anybody." I'm the closest person to Billy Joe, and he starts waving it around. In that moment I thought, *Billy Joe Shaver's crazy ass is about to taser me as a joke.* He didn't. It was a close call.[20]

Brian Wright at the Basement East, Nashville, Tennessee, September, 2017. Photo by Mark Whitified Lennon.

Brian Wright was born in McLennan County, Texas, and began writing songs at age thirteen. Wright started his career playing bars around Austin and Dallas until moving to Los Angeles in 2002, where he formed the band Brian Wright and the Waco Tragedies, regularly playing at the Hotel Cafe in Hollywood. In 2006, he released his folky debut, Dog Ears. *In 2011 Wright signed to Sugar Hill Records and released two albums on the label,* House on Fire *(2011) and* Rattle Their Chains *(2013). Wright currently lives in Nashville and is co-owner of the label Cafe Rooster Records alongside his wife, singer-songwriter Sally Jaye.*

Wayne Hancock

Billy Joe Shaver is a folk hero. He got in that scrape with the guy in [Lorena], and one thing led to another. The guy followed him outside, and Billy Joe ended up shooting him. I wouldn't want to do it myself, but I like it. The fact that he [did] that and stayed out of prison is just a testament to [the] kind of guy he is. A lot of people could have done it and would not have done as well as he did. The good Lord must love

Wayne Hancock, Abilene Bar & Lounge, Rochester, New York, September 2018.

him a lot, because when he shot the fella, he shot him right in his head, through the cheeks. I was surprised by it, because he's a warm human being. Then again, I've never pissed him off.

Billy Joe is a friend of mine. We've been friends for a long time. He's always been a straight up, laid back, cool cat, with a no-shit personality. No frills, just go, [a] bare bones, stand-up guy. I used to open shows for him, and he's always been very nice to me. I started out playing for some of these bigger names, and sometimes they're having a bad day or they're snobby. Half of them don't even come out and acknowledge you onstage. Billy Joe Shaver is always different from that. He comes out and watches the band play. If he likes your music, he'll tell you. It says a lot about him as a person. He's a professional. He's never political, and he never talks down to anybody.

Billy Joe is a prolific songwriter. He's a survivor. He writes from the heart. His songs are down-to-earth and approachable. They match his personality. He's an outstanding performer because he's a storyteller. He takes you on a journey with his songs. He heals the audience. A lot of guys won't play honky-tonks. They've got to have big money and a five-hundred-person room. Honky-tonks are where the working-class people are. He performs for the people who love his music. It's a tribute to him. Regardless of his music, the way he is makes me a fan. I hope that in twenty years I can be as good of a guy as he is. I respect the hell out of him.[21]

Wayne Hancock, born Thomas Wayne Hancock III, on May 1, 1965, was given the nickname Wayne "The Train" because of his powerful vocal style that hearkens back to Hank Williams Sr. With his debut album, Thunderstorms and Neon Signs, *Hancock created a new sound, Juke Joint Swing, that is a mix of thirties jazz, rockabilly, and traditional honky-tonk. Hancock has influenced artists of today such as Pokey LaFarge and Hank Williams III who recorded three of Hancock's songs on his 1999 solo debut* Risin' Outlaw, *"Thunderstorms and Neon Signs," "Juke Joint Jumping," and "Why Don't You Leave Me Alone." Hancock has recorded eight studio albums, including* Ride *(2013), which made it to number sixty-eight on the* Billboard *Country Albums chart. Hancock is the recipient of two Ameripolitan Music Awards, winning Best Honky Tonk Male in 2014 and Best Rockabilly Male in 2016.*

Tim Easton

I first saw Shaver in Columbus, Ohio, with about six other people at a bar called Stash's. Eddy was still with him. . . . I was in college, and it was my first real face-to-face example of Texas country music. He's like a big brick wall standing there. I'd never seen anything like it. I've never seen a performer that just stood there and delivered. I always thought he was better stripped down than with a big sound behind him, but he's used to playing honky-tonks where the audience is somewhat unbearable to the acoustic performers. But the songs speak for themselves. He's an ass kicker, that's what he does. Townes and Guy were more the poet spirits. He's the shitkicker living the life of a Texan who also happens to write songs. Those guys were songwriters who happen to be Texans and might enjoy a conversation about the craft of songwriting. Billy Joe could probably give two shits and would rather talk about farming.

I learned from Billy Joe to keep it simple and to rerecord your songs if you want to. I remember record company guys talking, "He's just going to rerecord these songs and put them on a different label with a different vibe." I thought, Why not? I don't do it with all my tunes, but I have no problem rerecording something if it didn't pop off the way I needed it

Left to right: Will Sexton, Tim Easton, JT Van Zandt, Catfish Concerts, Austin, Texas, March 16, 2014. Photo by Brian T. Atkinson

to. It's like bringing the jazz and folk method into country songwriting. Townes Van Zandt did the same thing.

I should have met Billy [for the first time] in Cleveland, Ohio. I was supposed to play a show with him and Willie Nelson. Billy Joe was second, but he canceled, so I got bumped up [and took his spot]. It was a snowy night, and the radio announcers had gotten the audience pumped up. As I took the stage, the audience is chanting, "Willie! Willie!" I just plugged in my electric guitar and shredded it. I sawed their heads off the best I could and actually converted that audience. It led to me getting a record deal.

When I was on New West Records with Billy Joe and Jon Dee Graham, I wound up in a car with [Billy Joe] going from the airport in Denver, Colorado, up to Boulder to play a radio conference with them. It was a songwriters-in-the-round sort of thing. Billy Joe was in a pretty good mood, but I don't think he wanted to do the in-the-round, but it was already established that's what it was going to be, so he didn't fight it. On the way up there, the ride was pretty much dominated by stories of him partying up there in the seventies. He remembers running into guys that were taking a lot of drugs. He didn't say what he was up to at the time. He left that open, but he told some funny stories about being there in Colorado. During the performance, he called out for me to do a solo thing on one of his songs. He was cordial to us songwriters. He knew he was in a mentor position.

Later on, I opened for him at Antone's in Austin in 2013, and he was more abrasive. It was after the shooting. He was funny about it, but he was in that "If you don't love Jesus, go to Hell" mode. I just stood there and thought to myself, *I don't think that's the way Jesus would do it. That's your way. You wanna hit 'em over the head?* I get it. He's a legend to us. His character comes with these stories that already precede him. You accept it, stand back, and don't interrupt him. Let him talk. Plenty of people have called Shaver the real deal. He is. When I first met him in the late nineties, he didn't even have a phone. Cameron Strang told me about it. He ran New West, signed Billy Joe, and is partly responsible for his resurgence. In order to get a hold of Billy, you'd have to call a gas station and leave a message for him. Sometimes in Texas the old guys hang, get coffee, and shoot the shit at these gas stations. That's exactly what it was. So if you wanted to talk to Billy, you'd have to call some gas station. Recently, I saw him play at the Country Music Hall of Fame show with Jessi Colter and others. Onstage, he said his car broke down. I thought, *Well if there's one real outlaw here tonight, that's the guy.*[22]

Tim Easton, born April 25, 1966, in Lewiston, New York, but raised in Akron, Ohio, formed the band the Kosher Spears while in college, then traveled the world. Upon his return to the United States, Easton joined the Haynes Boys who released Guardian Angel *in 1996. Easton signed with New West Records in 2001 as a solo artist, releasing the album* The Truth about Us *and then critically acclaimed follow-ups* Break Your Mother's Heart *(2003),* Ammunition *(2006), and* Porcupine *(2009). After his departure from New West, Easton released five more studio albums from 2011 to 2019, including the Sun Records–inspired* Not Cool *(2013), which he began recording after he moving to back to Nashville, where he now resides.*

Get Thee behind Me, Satan

Then saith Jesus unto him, Get thee hence, Satan: for it is written, Thou shalt worship the Lord thy God, and him only shalt thou serve. —Matt. 4:10

Michael Ubaldini

I discovered Billy Joe Shaver's music in a used record bin years ago. I went in to get *Give 'em Enough Rope by* the Clash, who were new at the time, but I loved country music my entire life and grabbed *Honky Tonk Heroes on* a whim for fifty cents. Both those records resonated and hit me the same way. No compromise. When I found out Billy Joe wrote the songs, I dug deeper. His songs are so complete. Honest with a hint of recklessness. It drew me in.

I've always dug gospel music. I really got into Billy Joe through his gospel records. Those run deep for me. I've had a lot of tragedy in life, but my faith in God always pulls me through. Shaver was cool like Hank Williams and Johnny Cash. Usually when someone sings that type of music they seem unhip. Not them. With Shaver, I felt like I had an ally. If someone tries to be witty and rip Jesus like the song "She left me for Jesus," where [Hayes Carll] says "If I ever find Jesus, I'm kicking his ass," Billy's answer would be, "If you don't love Jesus, go to Hell." Conformists don't dig God. Nonconformists do. And if you think you could kick Shaver's ass? It ain't gonna happen. He lets you know in the song that

Michael Ubaldini, promotional photo. Courtesy of Michael Ubaldini.

he's got Holy Ghost power. Stripped down bluesmen like Mississippi Fred McDowell and Charley Patton had songs like that too. "Get Thee behind Me, Satan" ranks with the best of Cash, Hank, Dylan's gospel albums, and the fire and brimstone African American preachers and singers.

I vividly remember seeing Billy Joe play at a bar in Arizona when I was touring. I walked back and read the sign twice, "Billy Joe Shaver here tonight." I thought, *Really? Here? It* was just a little bar. I went in and saw him play. People were talking. I couldn't believe it. Here's this great writer singing his songs, and people were gabbing away. The show was incredible. The people who listened to him got something great and inspiring. Those who didn't were just a backdrop on the canvas he was painting. That's why he's a honky-tonk hero.

When the show was over, I went back to my hotel room and started writing. He inspires a lot of my songwriting. He taught me to write what you believe in. There's no rules. You can write about what you live; booze, women, Gospel, protest, love, and hard times. Whatever is in your soul. He connects with people. He's real. He gets knocked down and gets back up. Like they say in boxing, "It's not how many times you knock out, it's what you do after you've been knocked down. Get up and find a way to win." His songs run through the blood of America and teach you that underdogs have something to offer and say. That's his legacy.[1]

Michael Ubaldini, born in Bayshore, New York, is a California-based award-winning alt-country singer-songwriter and published poet who mixes roots music with an against-the-grain attitude. The first song he learned was Hank Williams's "Jambalaya," which his dad taught to him at age seven. Michael is the founder of "Outlaws of Folk Music Series" and created a roots rock scene at the iconic Cuckoo's Nest punk rock club in Costa Mesa, California. He has recorded albums at Sun Studios and recorded for EMI with his former band, Mystery Train.

Aaron Watson

I remember one of the first shows I ever played with Billy Joe Shaver was in Odessa, Texas. Usually when we're done playing, we go down to sell merchandise. Instead, I went down to the front row and watched the whole show. I learned a lot. He's always got a smile on his face. He enjoys what he does. Regardless of what the industry was doing, he kept doing what he does. He's Johnny Cash, Kris Kristofferson, and Waylon Jennings rolled into one. He's a legendary outlaw, and he's always been very nice to me. I'm the same way with younger artists. I take the time to share things. I learned that from him.

I connect with Billy Joe with my love for Jesus. It's not religion. People like to say "spirituality," but that sounds like a medicine man. Billy Joe believes Jesus came to Earth not for the healthy but for the sick. Those who need him. I think a lot of people think Christians are these goody-two-shoe people that show up at church on Sunday mornings and then eat at Luby's after. Billy Joe gets out there in some rough and rowdy

Aaron Watson, Ryman Auditorium, Nashville, Tennessee, 2019. Photo by Zack Massey.

crowds, and he's always full of energy. He's got all the energy in the world, more than some twenty-year-old artists, and going to his concerts [is] like going to church and a honky-tonk at the same time. There's a lot of heart and soul. When you hear him singing his songs, you believe him.

We did a little gospel album [in 2007] called *Barbed Wire Halo,* and I thought it'd be cool to have the original honky-tonk hero read some Bible verses on it. When Billy Joe came in to read them, I had them all printed out, but he didn't even look at the sheet. He knew them by memory. It was amazing. The album came out the same week as the shooting in Lorena. I was doing interviews, and people asked, "What do you think about Billy Joe and the shooting?" I said, "Jesus loves everybody."

Billy Joe shares his gospel with millions of people. He's got Johnny Cash's swagger, and everyone can relate to "I'm Just an Old Chunk of Coal (but I'm Gonna Be a Diamond Someday)." He's up-front about his flaws and faith. He's not afraid to sing his songs about Jesus. I've always admired his boldness. It's incredible. There was a time when I was sitting in church, and this old cowboy came down and sat a few rows behind me. The preacher was preaching, and the guy started yelling. I could tell he'd been drinking, and everybody was frightened by the situation. He kept yelling, "I want to ask you something, preacher!" I walked back there, and I said, "Hey, let's go back here and we can talk." He said, "I don't want to talk to you. I want to talk to the preacher." I said, "Well, I promise you I have more interesting things to say." He kind of laughed at me. I took him into the back room next to the fellowship hall, and a couple of the guys from church came back too. We found out he had a wife who [had] died two years earlier, and that's when he started drinking. He'd been in jail for drinking and driving and just [gotten] out. He didn't have any money. They dumped him off at some halfway house where everybody's drinking. There were a bunch of elders from the church he didn't want to talk to. He didn't like them and didn't want them praying for him. He said, "I don't need your prayers. I'll pray for you." He was drunk, but he knew the Bible and said, "Well, I can quote you Jesus, and I can quote Waylon Jennings." I looked at him and [recited] the lyrics from [Shavers and Jennings's] "You Asked Me To," "Long ago and far away, in my old common labor shoes, I turned the world all which away, just because you asked me to." He completely changed. We were able to get him help and a place to stay that wasn't around alcohol. Billy Joe Shaver gave me street cred. He's rough around the edges, but I promise you he's brought as many people to love Jesus as Billy Graham.[2]

Aaron Watson, born August 20, 1977, in Amarillo, Texas, forged a slow and steady path to country stardom by both honoring tradition and embracing a more modern country sound. Watson released his debut album Singer/Songwriter *in 1999. His 2007 gospel record* Barbed Wire Halo *features Billy Joe Shaver reading Bible verses, and the album includes a cover of Shaver's "I'm Just an Old Chunk of Coal (but I'm Gonna Be a Diamond Someday)." Watson's 2015 album* The Underdog *reached number one on the Top Country Albums chart, and in 2017 he had his first major radio-play hit with "Outta Style." The title of his 2019 album* Red Bandana *symbolizes the American working class.*

Jason Charles Miller

I've lived in Los Angeles for seventeen years and connect with "L.A. Turnaround." Billy Joe is talking about worn-out souls and cold Los Angeles women. It still rings true. Being a country boy in L.A. makes me think of growing up, looking at the entertainment business, and looking at things differently out here. I always try to keep one foot back there and one foot here. I also love the sonics of the song. Kristofferson produced *Old Five and Dimers Like Me*, just like classic Kris. It's authentic

Jason Charles Miller tour poster. Photo by Courtney S. Lennon.

and raw. Those recordings move me because I feel like I'm listening to Billy Joe live, and I'm hearing it from every take. That's the vibe I get. I also love "Black Rose." It kicks off the album with this rock vibe, and he's singing about chickens and the first time he felt lightning because of the devil. It rings true. There's strength in the honesty and purity that I connect with. It makes me feel like I'm listening to a guy who lived the songs. Tragedy happened to him. Getting his fingers cut off and things that happened later. It's like he was a soothsayer for his own life. He's coming from pure intent and never strayed.

I've gone on a spiritual journey throughout my life. I went through some different phases. I grew up in a casually Christian household. My parents were divorced when I was six. I spent more time with my mom. She was an Episcopal, and my dad, who I still saw on weekends, was Catholic. I went through a born-again period when I was eighteen, and then I studied Eastern religions like Buddhism. I'm somewhere on this cosmic spiritual ride, and the conclusion is to do good and avoid evil. Treat others as you'd want them to treat you. I have respect for everybody's religious beliefs and try not to infuse too much of my mine within it but at the same time leave hints here and there. I'm still on that journey, so I fully relate to Billy Joe. I love that he will unabashedly sing about his beliefs. I try to keep it ambiguous. He's a lot braver than I am.

I have a song on my [2018] album, *In the Wasteland,* called "Get Thee behind Me." As a writer, I've always gravitated toward Billy Joe's earlier stuff. I didn't realize he had a song in 2007 called, "Get Thee behind Me, Satan." It proves his influence through osmosis. "Get Thee behind Me" is from Pharisees and the Sadducees, when Satan was trying to repeatedly test Jesus. The devil was getting frustrated trying to turn him to sin. It's written from the devil's perspective. It's a different take. It's interesting how people react to the song. People that are very religious see it from one perspective, and people who aren't see it from another. I tried to thread the needle between the two.

Billy Joe's songwriting has taught me to not fear details. I love that his verses are descriptive, and the choruses are catchy. He'll write from the perspective of somebody that's already familiar. I think he'll assume that you know what he's talking about with certain things, because he's writing from his pure perspective. Oftentimes as songwriters, especially writing commercial releases, we want to write things that are as universally accepted as possible. We strive to write the next amazing song. "I'm going to write the next song that everyone in the world will sing along to." Billy Joe always wrote from his heart, and people were attracted to it. He didn't have the intent of writing a giant hit song. He had the [mind-set], "I'm going to write these songs. These are going to be from my point of view, and if you like them, great. If you don't? Oh, well." That proved to be way more successful than trying to write for the masses.

If you look at a forest, Billy Joe was one of the first trees of the outlaw movement. He was an acorn that grew into a mighty oak. He was a catalyst and made Texas country music what it is today. They didn't have the internet back in the early seventies, so if you're a casual fan, you don't know Billy Joe wrote nine of ten songs on *Honky Tonk Heroes*. People that are in the music business know the impact that Billy Joe Shaver had on songwriting, but I don't think the average music consumer does. You're consuming music, and you're going about your day. You buy the Waylon Jennings record, and you think he wrote these songs he's singing and that they're about him.

It's important Billy Joe's music stays alive for future generations, because he's a piece of human history. He's a piece of what was happening in music at that time. He changed it, moved the bar, and pushed the envelope. It's important for people to hear his songs to know that something was happening outside of the norm. People reacted so strongly, and the outlaw movement changed the way country music was viewed, produced, written, and presented. It's extremely important for people to still be taught and know that. I really admire Billy Joe. He's an unsung hero.[3]

Jason Charles Miller, born January 5, 1972, in Cheverly, Maryland, grew up in Clifton, Virginia, where he started out performing at the age of six, singing opera and playing guitar. Miller is the front man of the industrial rock band Godhead, the only band signed to Marilyn Manson's Posthuman Records. After a decade with Godhead, Miller began to create music as a solo artist. In 2001, he moved to Los Angeles where he opened his own studio and works as a recording artist, writer, producer, and voice-over actor. Miller's solo music is inspired by his country roots, and his first single, "You Get What You Pay For," appeared in the HBO hit series True Blood.

Miller has been featured in magazines such as Rolling Stone, Billboard, *and* Guitar World. *He has appeared on MTV, MTV2, and VH1. Miller is half the band The Deadly Grind, who released their debut album,* Songs from ForeverVerse, *in 2017.*

Brennen Leigh

Billy Joe Shaver is an old-school, Texas-into-Nashville guy who has all the strengths of a great songwriter. His songs are completely unique in every way, with natural vernacular and honesty. He doesn't put on any airs. No songwriter needs flowery stuff, just natural speech the way that human beings communicate. You can count a lot of people in country music that write or wrote very intelligently with very little education as we know it. Hank Williams was not the most educated man, yet he was an incredibly intelligent songwriter. Billy Joe isn't lazy or clumsy. He goes back and edits. He puts a lot of thought into it and he would never sing anything he wouldn't say. He's authentic and does what he wants.

I first met Billy Joe when I was nineteen and [had] just moved to Austin from Fargo, North Dakota. Someone gave him a copy of one of my records. He called me on the phone. It came out of nowhere, and

Left to right: Brennen Leigh, Sophia Johnson, and Sunny Sweeney, Catfish Concerts, Austin, Texas, January 10, 2016. Photo by Brian T. Atkinson.

he left a message I'll never forget. He said, "Hi, Brennen. This is Billy Joe Shaver. I hope you remember me." And [he] went on to tell me how much he liked the record. It gave me an ego boost. I hadn't really learned how to write songs yet, and he was giving me kindness. It was interesting to me, because I'm this young songwriter, and he's Billy Joe Shaver. Shortly after that, I was with him, and he said, "Oh. You're just a baby." We were with my brother, and [Billy Joe] says, "She's good. Don't let her get married and get pregnant." At the time, I thought, *How completely none of your business that is.* It stuck with me, and now it rings true. It wasn't his business, but he knew the way that things could go for somebody like me. He's always struck me as a sweet country person. I know there's another side of his personality, but I've only seen the gentle side of him that comes out of his love for the world, for God, and music.

Seeing Billy Joe play is spiritual. He's an unbridled, magnetic performer who dances full of the Holy Spirit with a heavenly band behind him, straddling the barroom barrelhouse rock and roll with how country he is. I tend to lean hard-core country with my faith, growing up on gospel and bluegrass. Billy Joe's influenced me with the beats he creates in his songs like "Black Rose" or "Honky Tonk Heroes." It's a slightly crazy, groovy, delicious vibe few are capable of. Just perfect. I'm not much of a rocker, but I'll be damned if Billy Joe doesn't get me moving. He's one of the few people who can get up there and just sing without an instrument and not look like a big dork. I'm envious. He doesn't play guitar. Everyone knows he can. If you're a woman and you don't play guitar, people assume you can't. Maybe one day when I'm his age, I'll quit playing, dance around, and be so cool. He's a force. I love the guy.[4]

Brennen Leigh is a Nashville-based singer-songwriter and multi-instrumentalist who has written songs for artists including Lee Ann Womack, Rodney Crowell, Sunny Sweeney, Charley Crockett, Sarah Borges, and Whitney Rose. In 2013, Leigh released the Gurf Morlix–produced Before the World Was Made with her frequent songwriting and touring partner Noel McKay. Leigh was a core member of country bluegrass band High Plains Jamboree from 2015 to 2017, also featuring fiddler Beth Chrisman, McKay on guitar and vocals, and bassist and banjo player Simon Flory. Her 2015 album Brennen Leigh Sings Lefty Frizzell *is a tribute to Texas honky-tonk pioneer, Lefty Frizzell.*

Bonnie Montgomery

Every time I've seen Billy Joe play, it's been a spiritual experience. When he's entertaining you, you can tell every cell of his body was born for it. He's connected to the spiritual realm. It might be because of his life and loss, but you can see he has one foot in the other world. I can see light around people. The light around him is bright and beautiful. He's superhuman.

The first time I met him was 2013, opening for him at the Whitewater Tavern [in Little Rock, Arkansas]. Upstage at the Whitewater, you can see the stage through the cracks of the floor. On the first night, he sat there during my set and listened. He had on a red sequin jacket. He looked classy. I felt like there was an angel standing above me. After I played, we were taking photos with him backstage. He's always coming out of the hospital to shows. He said, "Hold me up, girls," and we did. He's smiling and loving every minute of it. He's very generous. In the middle of it, he stopped everything, put his hand on my head and said,

Bonnie Montgomery (*far left*) and friends hanging at the Whitewater in Little Rock, Arkansas with Billy Joe Shaver.

"You got the gift, girl. I don't know what you're gonna do with it, that's up to you, but you've got the gift." I had this flood of energy go all the way down my body. He has such a strong presence of character and an overload of personality. I felt like it was a blessing from a high priest. It was one of the biggest successes of my life. Bigger than any record label or industry moment. I could die a happy woman.

Billy Joe touches into a universal feeling that everyone can relate to with his songs, and the specifics about the people and places are poignant and unforgettable. "Live Forever" is gorgeous, and I identify with it because I've lost a lot of people I love. I've seen things that allude to the other realm. That song is so close to the idea of an afterlife.

I've never sat down to write a song like him, but it's so important in my mind and soul that it comes out. He's influenced me with the ease of his lyrics and the simplicity of the stories he tells. It's an art. I think it will be different in the future, because the world is becoming so different. We don't pass down knowledge through stories as much as we used to. Because now, there's so many other mediums, but his descriptions and firsthand accounts of life will stand out to the generations coming up behind us.[5]

Bonnie Montgomery is a native of Arkansas who was classically trained as an opera singer. Following country and bluegrass tradition, Montgomery holds the Outlaw Female title from the 2016 Ameripolitan Awards as well as the Americana Artist and Female Vocalist titles from the 2018 Arkansas Country Music Awards. Montgomery toured extensively in support of her 2018 album, Forever, *including a continuous run with Ray Wylie Hubbard. Her 2019 single "You Can't Shake" is a fiery collaboration with singer-songwriter and guitarist Rosie Flores.*

Salt of the Earth

Roger Alan Wade

Billy Joe Shaver is William Faulkner writing country songs. There's not a finer songwriter to wear a pair of boots. It's unfair to compare him to anyone else, because he's on a level of his own and has maintained that through the years. He's a thoroughbred whose writing and singing are holy beyond religion and as worldly as a cathouse jukebox. He made the outlaw movement happen with art and integrity. He's not doing it as a hobby. He's not doing it to get rich or because it beats roofing houses and paving highways. It's what he was born to do. He writes like wild horses run, and his songs hit you from every angle. There's no smoke and mirrors. No tricks. He lays it right out there. It looks simple on the surface, but there's only a few cats that can write at that level: Shakespeare, Willie Nelson, and Billy Joe Shaver.

My favorite singers are Willie Nelson, Bob Dylan, Billy Joe Shaver, and Waylon Jennings. Cats that communicate. I don't care about all the vocal gymnastics and the fancy stuff. It's about telling stories. Nobody does it better than Billy Joe Shaver. His performances are like a tent revival. You know there's passion and an hallelujah [factor] that's so compelling and takes it to the marrow. There's no pretention whatsoever. He goes skinny-dipping in his soul, and you're going to witness a Pentecostal honky-tonk jubilee. It's an experience.

Back in the eighties, when I was a hillbilly kid from Chattanooga, Tennessee, who [had] just moved to Nashville, we drank in the same old bars, but I never had the nerve to approach him. He was like Elvis to

Roger Alan Wade.
Photo by Winker.

me. Late one night, he was bummed out and wondering if it'd be okay for him to go over to some studio and pitch songs to one of these hot, flavor-of-the-month bands. I was freaking out, bug-eyed, and started talking to him, "Man, you're fricking Billy Joe Shaver. You could pitch songs to Sinatra, or Elvis, or the Beatles, or the Rolling Stones. Waylon Jennings. You already had Waylon Jennings cut your songs. Why would you back down from anything?"

I've always admired Billy Joe, and, just a little bit later, I got lucky. Hank Jr. recorded my song "Country State of Mind." It went to number one, so I had to go to the BMI Awards, which was this big bunch of ballyhoo. You've got to dress up, and they give you a certificate and this medallion on a red ribbon to wear around your neck. I went over and got mine. I had my ex-wife with me. I told her, "I know where I'm going with this." She said, "What are you going to do?" "I'm taking it to Billy Joe." I knew he'd be over there drinking. She got me a magic marker, and I signed that red ribbon that held the medallion. It said, "From Roger Alan Wade, to Billy Joe Shaver. Thank you for being my hero." That's what he meant to me and still does. I took it over there to him. He knew what it was. He'd been there before. He was so sweet and humble about it and gave me good advice. If I didn't take it, I'd probably have gotten killed. He said, "Son, I appreciate this, but you need to take that to your mama." I did, and, all these years later, she's still got it hanging on her wall.

Billy Joe has been an inspiration. I learned that a song can mean a thousand different things to a thousand different people and to trust the listener to get it. Billy Joe isn't trying to pontificate or preach to us. He's just writing as true and honest as he can. Ernest Hemingway wrote like Billy Joe. He'd be writing Nick Adams stories about a trout swimming against the current. How the bottom of the river would change and how the sunlight would hit the water. Then there's all these intellectuals who are pompous asses and read into all that stuff . . . what he meant. He's just writing about fish. Same with Billy Joe. He's excellent, and picking your favorite song is like picking your favorite child.

"Ride Me Down Easy" is the ultimate highway song. I love "Hill Country Love Song" off *Salt of the Earth* because it's so simple, sweet, precious, and honest. I love "You Asked Me To" for the same reason. He has a song called "The Real Deal." If anybody else wrote that, it'd sound like bragging, but Billy Joe's telling the truth. He's the real deal. There ain't no bullshit about him. You immediately have the sense that this isn't a man to be toyed with. This isn't a man to approach in any way but with respect. You get back what you give. You wouldn't want to go at him with bad intentions. You'd probably wind up spending a few days in the hospital.

So many get caught up on these trends and the fashion of the day. What's selling and what isn't. Billy Joe Shaver songs aren't being written in beige cubicles. He is an outlaw and not in a boardroom. His body of work isn't beholden to charts and trends. I think he found the secret of poetry in the same place Ben Hogan found the secret of the golf swing, the Texas dirt. They both come from hardscrabble background. I'm not much of a golfer, but I've always admired Ben Hogan. He was a no B.S. guy like Billy Joe. They asked him one time what his secret was and where he found it, and he just said, "I found it in the dirt," which meant he just worked all the time at it.

My grandson Roland Dixon is amazingly talented, and the first thing I told him is to listen to Billy Joe Shaver. That's what it means to me. Generation after generation should do that the way we now listen to Robert Johnson and Mozart. The rest of the stuff comes and goes, but those cats were built to last. It's the [difference] between literature and romance novels. Paperbacks run up and down the charts and you never hear of them again. Billy Joe's songs ain't going nowhere. They are literature built for the ages, with that lasting ring of honesty, truth, and genuineness.

My cousin Johnny Knoxville is a huge Billy Joe Shaver fan, and we do a weekly radio show on the Sirius XM Outlaw Country channel. We play all the Billy Joe Shaver records we can. Johnny just adores him like I do. He's a true fan of country. I was looking forward to having Billy Joe on the Outlaw Country Cruise, but he got to the Tampa airport, got pissed at his band, fired them, and went back to Texas. It broke my heart, because I'm such a fan, but I ended up getting his room. Jack Temper from Sirius XM that puts it all together called me because there was a bunch of us piled in a room. He said, "Yeah. Billy Joe split, and went back to Texas. He's not going to be with us. So the good news is, we've got another room if you want his." I said, "Hell, yeah. That would be awesome."

What a blessing to have lived in the same time as Billy Joe Shaver. It would be like living in the time of Shakespeare and getting to see his plays, being able to cross paths with and experience him. We are just as lucky. If there's a Mount Rushmore for songwriters, he's the one that you carve into George Washington's spot. If you were in a foxhole in a real battle, he's one of the cats you'd pick to be in there with you. There ain't no back-down. If Billy Joe [had been] at the Alamo, things would have turned out different.[1]

Roger Alan Wade, born in Chattanooga, Tennessee, is an outlaw country troubadour who writes stripped-down songs that evoke hard luck, hard times, and blown chances. Wade worked as a songwriter in Nashville writing for artists including Johnny Cash, Waylon Jennings, and Hank Williams Jr. Wade also writes comedic songs, and he hosts the hour-long weekly show "Big Ass Happy Family Jubilee" on Sirius XM's Outlaw Country channel with Johnny Knoxville. Wade also writes comedically tinged songs like "If You're Gonna Be Dumb, You Gotta Be Tough" and "Butt Ugly Slut" from his 2005 album All Likkered Up.

Jonathan Tyler

Billy Joe Shaver is punk rock. He doesn't give a fuck. He's *Braveheart* and Mark Twain with rural Texas lingo. He's poetic American country with inherent understanding in an era when everyone's doing what they can to make extra money to get ahead. Billy Joe can't be bought or sold. If someone asks, "Can you come play this private party for some rich oil guys? They can't really pay ya, but come out and it'll be fun," he'd say, "Kiss my ass." It's beautiful, but it makes for a hard life.

Because of the commerce and big-business record industry being a huge thing, a lot of folk music and original country music wasn't a fame incentive. It was people hanging around after the bars closed, picking guitars, and playing songs with each other. That's how a lot of songs got passed down. You had a real love of music. Now, you've got Music Row and huge industries with office buildings that are making millions of dollars buying marble columns, all off musicians' backs, missing the point of what makes a great song and artist. Billy Joe is untouched. He's a hero of the working class and isn't fazed by the money grab. All the stories you hear make him sound like he's either the drunk at the bar and is there all the time or doesn't give a fuck about trying to further his position. I don't believe that he's not smart enough to understand how to take care of himself. He's just refused that way of life for something that's truer and more poetic. He doesn't play the game. He just wants to write incredible songs, and when his songs hit the mark, it's the best. He inspires me. He's my kindred spirit in attitude.

I didn't like country music growing up, but Billy Joe converted me. Years ago, I had to play guitar for Shooter Jennings at a show in Los Angeles. He wanted me to pick some songs. Most of the country stuff I know is songs from the nineties because I had a radio. I'm from a much younger generation and moved into the Texas scene as a rock and roll

Jonathan Tyler. Photo by Lindsay Roche.

guy in high school, but *Honky Tonk Heroes* won over my heart. It's my favorite country album of all time, how I became aware of Billy Joe, and why I started paying attention to his music. I could go through all that record, because it means so much to me. Every single one of those songs is perfect. It's a brilliant album. There's something about the way he talks, and the words that he puts in songs like "Old Five and Dimers Like Me." Only someone who lived it could write it, and I believe him when he sings. There's no phoniness. Picking your favorite Billy Joe Shaver song is like picking your favorite child, but I cover "Black Rose," which is probably my favorite. It's one of the first country songs that crossed the boundaries into rock and roll in the attitude and spirit.

I can watch Billy Joe Shaver perform and come out experiencing all these amazing songs that give me the strength to keep going. His songs, and what he's done, [are] more beautiful than the commercialization and homogenization of music for the purpose of selling more records that's continually degrading the quality to make more money. I'd rather hear somebody who is writing songs that really mean something. Billy

Joe does that. He doesn't care about the bullshit. He was supposed to be on the Outlaw Country Cruise a few years ago. He pulled all the way out to [the dock], and he said, "Nah. Never mind. I'm good. I'm going home." When everybody else is bending the knee to the queen, Billy Joe is irreverent. It's something that's lost in this day and age, but Billy Joe does what he wants. I love that about him. He's a character out of the movies. He deserves to have a book written about him.[2]

Jonathan Tyler, born in Dallas, founded Jonathan Tyler and the Northern Lights in 2007. Shortly after, the band went into the studio and recorded their debut Hot Trottin' *with local producer Chris Bell. By 2008, the band began touring in support of major acts like Erykah Badu, Leon Russell, Deep Purple, the Black Crowes, and Chicago. In 2008, the band was discovered at South by Southwest by an A&R representative from Atlantic Records. They soon were signed to the label's F-Stop imprint and released their 2010 album* Pardon Me. *The title track went to number twenty-seven on the* Billboard *country singles chart. Tyler's 2015 album* Holy Smokes *was released on Timeless Echo.*

Jackson Taylor (Jackson Taylor and the Sinners)

Billy Joe Shaver is country music's Charles Bukowski. He brought street-level grittiness with lyrics and melody that are number one. He's very precise and sparing with words. He doesn't throw them around. He's a complete artist. Top-tier. If it wasn't for him, I wouldn't be doing what I'm doing. My dad was a big fan, and, [when I was] growing up, he and my uncles would start drinking and put on Billy Joe records. So that's what I was going to emulate. I really can't tell you where I end and Billy Joe Shaver starts. He's one of my biggest influences as a songwriter and human. When my band did a video for "Honky Tonk Heroes," he came out for it. His van was packed up with a bunch a stuff, and his guitar was sitting there, and everything was real. At the time, he was going through a situation. He shot a guy in the face. He's John Wayne, and for him to do the video is a testament to how generous he is. He always has been. It blows my mind.

I've played a lot with Billy Joe and started out running sound for him. With his shows, I wouldn't call him a performer. He's entertaining, but

Jackson Taylor, promotional photo. Courtesy of Stefani Moretti.

he isn't putting it on for effect. Justin Timberlake, Garth Brooks, and Dwight Yoakam do great shows, but you can tell they put a lot of time and rehearsal into it. Billy Joe doesn't. He's a preacher testifying, and he's so honest he can make me uncomfortable. There's nothing fake about him. From the first time we hung out, he was cool and authentic. It was in Nashville at a little place on Broadway that got knocked down when a tornado came through in 1997. I met him in the bathroom. Very approachable. I [told him that] "Ain't No God in Mexico" is my favorite song and what an honor it was to meet him. He was so kind and gracious, completely unaware of who he is, what he represents, and what he's created.

One time I was opening for him in Texas, and he showed up with a guitar in this beautiful coffin case. The guitar had bullet straps. He [had] stopped to get strings at Guitar Center [and seen] the guitar, said "that reminds me of Jackson," and picked it up. It wasn't a cheap guitar either. He just got it for me. I knew we were friendly, but I didn't think I was the type of person who would cross his mind if I wasn't standing there in front of him. I didn't think I was in his consciousness. It's one of the craziest things that's happened to me.

My life and views are unique compared to my peers. I grew up in poverty. I was a migrant farmworker. He grew up in a similar way. Listen to "Ride Me Down Easy," that's him broke down on a highway. If it hasn't happened to you, you're not going to relate. There are hipsters whose friends turned them onto Billy Joe, but you're going to have to have lived life to a certain degree to really relate to him. The people I find who really love him come from that same mold and know what his lyrics mean. There are not enough people who know what it's like to really bond with Billy Joe in the way I and others do.

Billy Joe was never indicative of any type of country music, and I don't think rock music or country music could claim him. He was always different. We'd talk about music from the 1960s and 1970s. He hasn't changed much. Country music hasn't changed much. Of course, there's always been guys who have come along and changed country music—Hank Williams, Ernest Tubb, Buck Owens, and Lefty Frizzell—but the very top part of country music has always been awful, and the softer people get, the more offended they get. You hear people singing about being badasses, and that they stick to what they believe in, but they never fucking tell you what they believe, and they never tell you what they are. They sing songs about who they are, but they don't say anything about it. Billy Joe Shaver never does that, but you know exactly what kind of person he is when you hear him. He doesn't have to tell you. Either you know what his lyrics mean, or you don't.

When Billy Joe goes and makes a record or writes a song, he's not trying to fit into any mold or category. That's why his music is covered by so many people without becoming big hits. I don't think anyone has as many cuts as Billy Joe Shaver without them being huge hits. It says something about him. If you're cutting a record and put your money into it, you have to put a lot of thought into it because you've only got so many songs on a record. People keep recording his songs because even if they don't have a track record of being hits, they mean something. I think that says a lot. There's always going to be people cutting Billy Joe Shaver songs as long as there's people who have been down on their luck, gone to the edge, and stood on it and made it back. He'll always have fans like me who will drive nine hours to see him, who think he's the best. When people find him, they love him.

Billy Joe's legacy is survival. Legacies are all different. His legacy [is] individual. You have people who become part of the public consciousness, but Billy Joe's not [like that]. Growing up, I didn't know that. I thought he was as big as Elvis, huge everywhere, but he's always been underground, because we just have a way-too-pampered society. I wish the whole world could see Billy Joe Shaver for what he is. He's one of America's greatest poets. He's his own entity.[3]

Jackson Taylor is the Denver-based front man for the outlaw country band Jackson Taylor and the Sinners. Taylor spent his youth growing up and working as a migrant farmworker in California and Washington. In 2001, Taylor began his career as a recording artist and has since independently released over a dozen albums with multiple appearances on Billboard's Top 100 Singles *charts. Billy Joe Shaver says, "['Hard to Be an Outlaw'] came from one of the wild conversations with my roughhouse, rounder, one and only, real brother. Far as I'm concerned, straight shooting, greatest entertainer, songwriter, kickass, lives life to the hilt, outlaw who ever lived—or will live—my best friend, Jackson Taylor."*

Stoney LaRue

The first time I met Billy Joe was fifteen years ago at Willie's Fourth of July Picnic. I was eating tacos over by my van and offered him one. He said, "Sure." We sat there eating tacos and talking bullshit. We later played together at this place Hat Tricks in Lewisville, Texas. I didn't know he would recognize me, because that's the way it goes out there on the road, especially with people you look up to. I was in the crowd. He's playing, and says, "I'm glad to see everybody here this evening, and I want to get one of my good friends, Stoney LaRue up here." I was thinking, *What the hell?* I was in the crowd, not expecting to get up there. I love how he just threw me into the fire. It was a sink or swim kind of thing. He's very generous. I think if he sees that you're not full of shit, he's into it, but he can probably smell that coming from a mile away. He's very fatherly, genuine, and lets you know that you're doing the right thing. Every time we see each other, it's kind of picking up where we left off. I [saw] him in Nashville at Exit/In. I went backstage, and he

Stoney LaRue. Photo by Richard Arp-Barnett, courtesy of RPR Media.

was taking his heart pills, chewing on his nitroglycerin. I said, "Whoa, man, you need all those?" He goes, "Don't you talk to me about my pills." I was like, "Okay. I'm just asking you." "I'm good. See you out there."

"Honky Tonk Heroes" always sticks out to me. I recorded it on Waylon's tribute album down in New Braunfels years ago with Shooter and Jessi. When you're with Billy, you don't [necessarily] realize that he's one of the smartest people in the world, because it's so easy. When I'm writing songs, Billy Joe is somewhere in the subcochlear region of my brain saying, "Simplicity is always a good way." That's why his songs are so beautiful. They're poetry.[4]

Stoney LaRue was born in Taft, Texas, but raised in Buffalo Valley, Oklahoma. He moved to Stillwater, Oklahoma, where he befriended fellow red dirt artists Jason Boland and Cody Canada, and the three moved into "the yellow house" together, where they would have late-night jam sessions and entertain other musicians around the town, such as Mike McClure and Brandon Jenkins. LaRue was heavily influenced by Woody Guthrie, Bob Childers, Mike Hosty, and the red dirt music scene. LaRue fronted the Organic Boogie Band and released the album Downtown *in 2002, recorded at Cain's Ballroom in Tulsa. His solo follow-up,* The Red Dirt Album, *charted at number seventy on the* Billboard Country Albums *chart, and his subsequent studio albums,* Velvet *(2011),* Aviator *(2014), and* Us Time *(2015) all made it into the top forty. LaRue often cowrites with Texas singer-songwriter Mando Saenz.*

Matt Harlan

I got into Billy Joe's music when I moved to Houston in 2005. I had a friend that worked at Compadre Records. [Billy Joe] was on the label. She used to glowingly talk about him. I was already hearing about him through others as I was getting into acoustic music for the first time as a player, discovering [songwriters like] Joe Ely, Guy Clark, Todd Snider, and Robert Earl Keen. I have a habit of getting into whatever people find as influences and search[ing] it out. I like to know where things come from. So it was just a matter of time before I found him.

The first time I saw Billy Joe live was in Austin at the Continental Club. He was doing a benefit for Kinky Friedman's [dog] rescue organization and wasn't playing with a band frequently, so he didn't bring one. He was playing by himself. I'd heard his songs by then, and I was really excited to see him. I didn't really care in what way. He was fumbling around a little bit playing the guitar, because he hardly has any fingers on that one hand. I was shocked that he managed to do anything in the first place. Then he was having a lot of trouble and stopped playing guitar, but he didn't stop the show. He said, "Okay. Fuck this. I'm going to sing a capella." And he did. He sang all of these songs I [had] started to love. Looking back, I love them even more. It was powerful. Him sitting there clapping and waving his arms like an angel. It was a [big] moment for me at a time when I was trying to figure stuff out. He taught me how to keep going when things are really tough. How to have confidence in yourself and give it your all.

I first met him when I was starting out. I played a show with him in 2008 at Courville's in Beaumont, Texas. People who didn't even really know him seemed to be moved by the show. I played a show with him right after he got his knee operated on, which was pretty crazy. He did the exact same show I've seen him do dozens of other times. He was just taken by the whole experience, and he gave way more than a lot of people

Matt Harlan, Live Oak Cemetery, near Blaze Foley's headstone, Manchaca, Texas, January 13, 2019. Photo by Brian T. Atkinson.

give. He's a ball of energy and always comes off the stage totally soaked and still hugging on folks and just energized from going up there. Every time I've [played] with him, he's been super nice, hugging me, and just being real. I have some friends in Houston who played with him quite a while, and they've always had great things to say about him. I've heard some folks say funny stuff before, like he'll kick people out of his band if they get too good, so he doesn't have to pay them a whole bunch, but he's always been great when I've seen him. It's not just about musicians. He taught me and a lot of other people how to be nice to an audience.

Billy Joe's made an impact on so many people. He's a direct tie to a time of life and a style that people just imitate now. Folks want to see someone who actually was the figure that a lot of folks write and sing about. His role in the outlaw movement [was] huge. Anybody who can take one of the other leading figures in that movement and intimidate them into falling in love with and recording a whole album of his songs is bound to play a huge role, because it's about fucking the system and doing something different. He embodied the movement, going back to the roots [of country music] with purity. Those are tenets of it, and he brought a contradictory attitude. You have the rebelliousness, which was a huge part, but then the Christian and moral values side. He might go out and mess up because of the rebelliousness, but then [he] feels bad about it and goes and gets it right with God. He's a myth, and he's not dead.[5]

Matt Harlan, born in Boerne, Texas, is a critically acclaimed Houston-based singer-songwriter who has performed all over the world, sharing stages with legendary songwriters including Guy Clark, Steve Earle, and James McMurtry, along with modern luminaries like Jamie Lin Wilson, Hayes Carll and John Fulbright. He was named singer-songwriter of the year in the 2013 Texas Music Awards and was featured alongside Lyle Lovett, Guy Clark, and others in the documentary For the Sake of the Song. *His 2019 album* Best Beasts *is marked with vivid vignettes that frequently feature blue-collar men struggling and sociopolitical narratives that are written with poetic elegance, through the artist's eye.*

Scott H. Biram

Billy Joe Shaver epitomizes stage presence with a real country voice. He could give David Lee Roth a run for his money. He flaps his arms like he's flying into heaven and really gets you. I saw him perform at a festival in Long Beach, California. I was playing with him. Me and my merch guy were standing there listening to him, and I said, "Man, I think I'm going to cry." He said, "Me too, man."

[Billy Joe was wearing] that same shirt he always wears. I'd like to know how many he's gone through or if it's the same shirt. I shook his hand, felt his stubs, and told him I was friends with Connie and Amy Nelson [because] they're good friends with him. He was just the nicest guy, the sweetest dude. Down to earth and completely appreciative of anyone saying thanks to him. It meant a lot to be around him, to be in his presence. I'm automatically connected to Billy Joe's music because of his Texas background. I grew up in the Texas country for the early part of my life. His music was just there. He's always come across as a [real] country person. I have a lot of respect for him in that way. He's one of the few legends left.

I felt bad for him [that night]. He'd tripped on his way back to the hotel before the show and had to go to the emergency room to get

Scott H. Biram, C-Boy's Heart & Soul, Austin, Texas, August 16, 2018. Photo by Brian T. Atkinson.

stitches and staples on his face. They had to put off the show a little while, and they had the band that was playing [after him] play before him. Then he got up there. He said, "It's gonna be a throbbin' night." He gave it his all.

Billy Joe's one of the biggest and has influenced a ton of artists. He belongs up there on the list with Willie, Waylon, and Bob Wills. He deserves more credit than he gets because his songwriting's like poetry, it's straight to the point, and paints the picture perfectly. He's not making an extreme effort to be poetic. It's built in him and just comes out. I get the feeling that he just shoots from the hip and effortlessly puts it to paper. Those lyrics seem to come from a pretty tight circle around the beating heart. There's a veil of down-home, redneck-ness over his words, but if you look through it, there's some profound content and humanness in his songs that people of different origins can relate to, straight-up country, what country is supposed to be.

I like to pride myself on thinking that I write straight from the heart, coming across as who I really am. I don't put too much relish on there. When people ask me about my own songwriting, I tell them I tend to write about the human condition. Billy Joe circles around the same thing, but he's ornery, and so am I. He's a Texas treasure. He blows my mind. I don't know if I'm going to shoot anybody in the face, but I think about it pretty often.[6]

Scott H. Biram, born April 4, 1974, in Lockhart, Texas, is an Austin-based acoustic blues punk rocker who started his career in punk band The Thangs and as a member of two bluegrass bands, Scott Biram & the Salt Peter Boys and Bluegrass Drive-by. Biram signed to Bloodshot Records in 2005, for whom he has released eight albums, from The Dirty Old One Man Band *through* Fever Dreams *(2020). He has shared stages with Willie Nelson, Shooter Jennings, Ryan Bingham, Roky Erikson, Hank Williams III, and Billy Joe Shaver.*

Gethen Jenkins

The last show I played with Billy Joe, I was opening for him at the Coach House in San Juan Capistrano, California. He'd finally got some good wheels. He pulls up in a bitchin' Sprinter van and jumps out. He was wearing his denim shirt like he always wears and had a Walmart bag full of water and Red Bull. He had road-worn, weary eyes, like he'd been trapped in the van for the last month. I was standing outside, and there's a gaggle of Los Angeles hipster kids, and whatever-the-fucks, waiting to get a glimpse of him or an interview. Billy walked by the kids, stood next to me, and I said, "How you holdin' out?" He said, "I'm gonna live, Big 'Un." He calls me Big 'Un. I asked, "Have you written me a hit yet?" He starts laughing, "I got this one song. I don't think you'd want to sing anything like this, but it goes like this, 'Don't give a damn worryin'; Don't care what I do; Don't know when I'm leavin' or where I'm going to; Sometimes I wear my cowboy hat; sometimes I wear my shoes; don't

Gethen Jenkins tour poster. Photo by Courtney S. Lennon

give a damn where I am; Don't care about what I do.' You wouldn't want to record anything like that would you?" "Hell, yeah, I would." "All right, you can have it and record it, but you gotta finish it." Meanwhile, the twenty-five other people had their jaws on the floor thinking, *Who the hell am I to be talking to Billy Joe Shaver?*

A little later, some rude blogger kid was eating up Billy's time. He'd just gotten there, and his dinner was ready to get served. It was about forty-five minutes into [the interview], and I finally walked in and said, "Hey, he's got to eat his dinner, you should probably let him go." So the kid left. As I was walking back, I said, "You ever listen to that song I wrote about me and you?" The song was "Honkytonk Life." I wrote it right after I'd gotten a call that I'd be opening for him the first time. He said, "No, I never heard it." "If you want to hear it, I'll play it quick." "All right." So I pulled my guitar out and played it. Billy gave me his undivided attention. He took his hat off. He was laughing at my words and hanging on my every note. It was a huge honor for me. He gave me his approval with his mannerisms and his own words. When I finished, he said, "Man, I wish I would have stolen that one," gave me a big hug, and went and ate his dinner. He's an encouraging guy. You couldn't possibly imagine. He takes time to talk to folks that are on different parts of their musical journey.

Billy Joe is the truth. He doesn't care what anyone thinks. He's brutally honest and open. He's a good ole boy. He doesn't try to act like a fancy, high-rolling, famous guy. He's just Billy Joe. He's humble, and he's willing to share a story, a hug, or handshake with anybody that's interested. He emotes love. He writes about what he's been through, painting a picture, and emoting with words and melody. He sacrifices himself. He cuts you to the bone. His songs are a glimpse of the light that is shining inside of him. It's magical. He's an amazing performer. He takes time to tell stories. He shows you a side of him that most performers don't have the courage to. There's no bullshit with Billy Joe Shaver, no fancy clothes. It's not about how many notes the guitar player can fit into a solo, it's about honesty. He opens his heart, but he's an ornery old cuss, and you don't want to cross him.

Billy Joe's music is going to be here a hundred years from now, because people don't write like that anymore. The music coming out now can't hold a candle to that honesty. Those songs are timeless. They move you. I did a cover of "When the Fallen Angels Fly," because the first time I heard it, it made me cry. If that song doesn't bring you to tears, you're fucking dead. No one writes like him. His songs will live forever, just like him.[7]

Gethen Jenkins, is a Huntington, West Virginia, native and award-winning singer-songwriter who was raised in Alaska and served eight years in the US Marines. Based in Southern California, Jenkins has shared the stage with artists such as the Marshall Tucker Band, Billy Joe Shaver, Wanda Jackson, and David Allan Coe. In 2017, he released his six-song EP, Where the Honkytonk Belongs, *earning regular play on Sirius XM Outlaw Country. He was honored with Male Vocalist of the Year and Album of the Year accolades at the 2017 California Country Awards. Jenkins was most recently named 2018's Best Outlaw Country Artist in* LA Weekly's *annual "Best of L.A." issue.*

Ben Reddell

No one can out-country Billy Joe Shaver. His rowdy honky-tonk lifestyle shook things up in Texas. I grew up in Kerrville. Between the Jimmie Rodgers Jubilee and the Kerrville Folk Festival, I saw a bunch of heavy hitters as a kid, and Billy Joe Shaver was one of them, but my love for country music didn't really come into fruition until I got to college. I was in Austin, going to bars on Sixth Street, later venturing down South Lamar and First Street to more country bars like the Broken Spoke and Horseshoe Lounge. Billy Joe's stories drew me in because they remind me of all the old-timers I grew up with in Texas. My cousin Noel McKay [who cowrote "El Coyote" with Guy Clark] has a song called "Disappearing Texas," which is about this lifestyle and the open land of our ancestors that's not as prevalent as it once was. Billy Joe embodies something that you just can't describe about being Texan. Something that just is. Every song is initially implied by him being a boy from around Waco. I try to write with that home influence he's mastered. I always look back on my twenties and wish I would have worked harder at being more productive. In my twenties, I just partied like my heroes,

Left to right: Billy Joe Shaver with Ben Reddell at Redwood Bar & Grill, Los Angeles, 2009. Photo courtesy of Ben Reddell.

yet I didn't really succeed like them. I didn't really get my stride until my thirties. When I was thirty, I had the pleasure of interviewing Billy Joe for a now-defunct magazine. I was working at a super corporate post house, snuck into the CEO's conference room, put Billy on speaker, and recorded it. We talked about everything from growing watermelons to belt buckles. A couple of years later, my band got to open for him here in Los Angeles. I played the song "Omaha." I love it, and he made it clear he doesn't, but it's the perfect example of his wit and simplicity. It's about a country boy wishing he was home. It's a beautiful lament with cowboy simplicity. Nothing fancy, nothing forced.

For me, just getting to talk to him and experience his larger-than-life presence in person gave me a confidence I lacked earlier in life. Billy Joe has [only an] eighth-grade education, but he's smart as hell, wild as hell, and authentic. I think what young musicians should learn from Billy Joe Shaver is to be proud of who you are and where you come from. Don't ever let some fancy fucker with an Ivy League degree make you feel he's better than you. Fuck him. Be who you want to be. That's Billy Joe's legacy.[8]

Ben Reddell, born July 5, 1980, in Kerrville, Texas, has lived in Los Angeles, playing in the local country music scene since 2003. Reddell is general manager of Bedrock Studios and creative director for the Grand Ole Echo.

Chris Fullerton

When I was seven years old, I started playing guitar because my mom and her entire side of the family played, all seven brothers and sisters, and my grandpa was the ringleader. They taught me Hank Williams songs, and that was all I knew until my teenage years hit, and then I was listening to hip-hop for a decade. I saw Billy Joe play at Waterloo [in Austin] when he was promoting [*Long in the Tooth*]. He had this campaign, "I rap on this album," and he kept going on about it. I searched for the album, and he's totally not rapping on it.

I first discovered Billy Joe's music when I was living in a friend's closet in Cambridge, New Jersey. It was right when Pandora came out. When my friend went to work, I'd go on his computer and listen to it. It would play, "If you like this, then you would like this." I was listening to Hank Williams, and "Ragged Old Truck" came on. I loved it, because it's a very open song. He talks about suicide jovially: I was gonna kill myself, but I shot the wall instead, then I went downtown and got fucked up. It's a little sexist, as are three-quarters of his catalog. I'm sure he's going for shock value.

After hearing the song, I went and got the album it was on, *I'm Just an Old Chunk of Coal (but I'm Gonna Be a Diamond Someday)*. It starts off with "Fit to Kill and Going Out in Style," then it goes into "Blue Texas Waltz," and you think, *What the fuck is this shit?* It's got these bangers, and then goes into these slow songs. That was the first time I got a taste of, "Oh, this is how they do it in honky-tonks? You play some crazy shit, then you play something three-quarters slower."

I think one of the first things that made me really dig him was watching a video after he'd just put out *The Real Deal*. It was supposed to be his comeback, so it had Big & Rich. They're taking the video in a nice house for him to promote it. He plays "No Fool Like an Old Fool," and it's just him talking about screwing this young girl in the house. She left him for an older guy. He could have played any other song, but he's just being honest. The music from the title track of my last record, *Epilepsy Blues*, was the sort of stuff I started playing [as I was] listening to him. There's a track on there called "Motel Blues," where I was thinking of him when I was playing because I was writing it, and I didn't care as much what I was saying.

"The Real Deal" is one of my favorite songs. He has this verse where he says, "I was out here working with a hoe, and we all know a hoe's not just a hoe anymore." He can't help but say whatever's in his head. He knows he's going to appeal to a hillbilly crowd. He's a very tactful songwriter, and he's very honest. "I'm Just an Old Chunk of Coal" is just perfect. He doesn't use his life as filler. He's really dedicated to finding the good path to be a good person. Then he'll do this thing where he'll have two super-sexist songs, and then he'll sing about Jesus. There are ones where the female in the song is a hero, like "Amtrak" [from his 1982 self-titled album], where she leaves and he's the one humiliated.

Chris Fullerton, South Austin, Texas, November 22, 2018. Photo by Brian T. Atkinson

She had to put all of her shit in a gunnysack. She's gone, and he wishes she wasn't. Sometimes he can be an asshole in that regard. In "Ragged Old Truck" he calls her a "heifer." I guess it's probably just the same sort of assertive male type who is comfortable calling themselves a feminist if you ask them, but really, they [only] feel comfortable having women [if] the women are working for them. I've seen him live a few times, and every time there's jokes about women who are standing right there. An ex-wife was at one of the shows, and he says, "Yeah, she's living with me again. I'm not putting it in any of her holes this time, though." Dude. She's standing right there.

As a performer, he gives it 100 percent. His band does a lot of the work, but he's really old. Seventy-nine years old, and he stands up there doing those crucifixion arms and waiting to die onstage. The last time I saw him, he had a fanny pack around his waist full of Red Bull and drank all ten of them onstage. I had no idea what was going on. I thought it was the greatest shtick in the world. Weirdest thing. He had another cooler off to the sides, and every once in a while, he'd take breaks, and the band would play something. The drummer was fucking nuts, and he'd take breaks and go refill Billy's stash. He should be sponsored by Red Bull. It's insane.

It's important Billy Joe's music is here in one hundred years, because, despite the jokes he makes, and my feminist perspective, I don't think he's a bad guy. He's a great gentleman. I think his music is good and that our country is in a bad place. We're going to need music from that section of the country to say, "Hey, these people weren't fucking assholes, they were making country music, and that was going on at a time when everything was falling apart." His legacy is going to be less about his hits and more about songs like "Hardworking Man" [from *Salt of the Earth*]. That'll be a Woody Guthrie-esque song when we're all alien laborers.

"Live Forever" always sticks with me. As a parent, the line "You fathers and you mothers, be good to one another, please try and raise your children right" makes you tear up and feel empowered. It's a song that lifts you up no matter where you are in life. As a songwriter, the best thing you can do is try to capture those moments that last. That's what makes a great song.[9]

Chris Fullerton, born December 29, 1985, in Camden, New Jersey, is a critically acclaimed Austin-based singer-songwriter whose debut album, Epilepsy Blues, *dealt with the feelings of depression stemming from the diagnosis of epilepsy he first faced as an adult. Fullerton's songs possess the lyrical depth and poetic prowess of Townes Van Zandt combined with the grit and maturity of early Delta bluesmen.*

Live Forever

John Rich (Big & Rich)

Billy Joe Shaver is a story in motion, an outlaw from a classic western, a Texas icon who can't be duplicated or replicated, with a voice like no one. He's brilliant, and his songwriting raised the bar to a level you can only hope to get close to. He's the ultimate country craftsman, with Johnny Cash and Merle Haggard, who gets across maximum information with minimal lyric. That's the trick as a songwriter. We aren't here to write books, we're here to write two-and-a-half minutes that impact you. Billy Joe's a master and has Waylon's energy. Only he can write a song like "I Been to Georgia on a Fast Train," and when it comes on, I crank it as loud as it will go.

I'm from Amarillo. Growing up in Texas, you're bound to hear Billy Joe. [Big Kenny and I] struck up an important friendship with him, sharing stages and on the road, outside honky-tonks at two in the morning listening to his crazy stories. You'll ask, "How did you lose your fingers?" "It was my second wife." He's hilarious. If you didn't know him you'd think he was making it up. I played "I'm Just an Old Chunk of Coal (but I'm Gonna Be a Diamond Someday)" last night at the Ryman, one of my all-time favorite songs. I asked him about it, and he said, "Yeah, that's a true story. I sat there and wrote it." Billy Joe is himself, not acting. He's authentic, genuine, and when you're around him he makes you go "I don't need to be anything but me." It's the same thing with Big & Rich. When Big Kenny and I are together things stretch outside the norm. Put the three of us together, and it's magic.

Left to right: John Rich and Big Kenny (Big & Rich), promotional photo. Courtesy of Wortman Works.

Billy Joe came to us to recut "Live Forever," saying he loved our harmonies, how our records sounded, and that he wanted us to produce it like a Big & Rich record. We said, "You kidding? You're never going to beat what you've done, but we'll take a shot." It was an honor to put our hands on his classic song and put a modern track around it. So, when ideas would come to us, we'd throw them at him. He says, "Do whatever's in your head." The song's about living, dying, and living forever after your death. We knew what we were doing would be permanent, so when we recorded the song, we pulled out all the stops. John and Martina McBride's Blackbird Studio in Nashville is one of the best in the world. Here's a guy in a multimillion-dollar room, rough as a Texas boot, saying, "Man. This is the fanciest studio I've ever seen." I said, "Nothing but the best for this song." We lived the song through the process. The vibe was ethereal.

"Live Forever" is a big celebration of life. The director of the video was Ricky Schroder from *Silver Spoons*. He's a fan of Big & Rich and Billy Joe

Shaver, so he had this great idea of setting it in a Tex-Mex town that combined our worlds. When all was said and done, it was Texas—so Billy Joe, so Big & Rich. The fans were blown away by the collaboration. We don't play the song every night, but, just about every show, college-age kids come up saying they saw the video and bought "Live Forever." It's cool. We mixed our audiences, and a lot of Big & Rich fans who didn't know Billy Joe Shaver did themselves a favor going down the rabbit hole of his music, and their lives are better for it.[1]

John Rich, born January 7, 1974, in Amarillo, began his songwriting career in 1992 as a member of the band Lone Star. In 2002, he formed the group Big & Rich with Big Kenny Alphin, and they signed with Warner Brothers in 2004. Their debut album Horse of a Different Color *includes the single* "Save a Horse, Ride a Cowboy" *and reached number one on the charts and went three times platinum. Through 2020, they have released six studio albums, five of which made it into the* Billboard Country Albums *top five, including the sixth,* Did It for the Party *(2017).*

Cory Morrow

I play "Live Forever" every night. It hit me off the bat. The melody is beautiful and simple. It was a few years before I found my faith. The song said a lot, and I really appreciate Eddy's take on it. They played in Austin quite a bit, so I'd go see them any chance I'd get. I loved the mix of Eddy's guitar and his influence on a song. I know that Billy loved it too. He'd always turn around, smile, and say, "Man, I never thought about that. That's cool."

Whenever I heard them play "Live Forever," I said, "Man, I want to play that, I want to start playing it. Give it justice. Give it my own thing, while honoring the original." I'm not one of these people that gets upset when people take departures in music. I think a long time ago, I got a little upset with Gary P. Nunn when he started playing "Homesick Blues" as a reggae song, [because] that's a severe departure from the original. He hardly ever played it the original way. For me, I love music, and it shouldn't be boxed in and labeled. We shouldn't be confined to playing a song the same way every time. Performing artists and musicians hit the road one hundred and two hundred days a year. You're going to play

Cory Morrow. Photo by Casen Hutton.

the same song every night and don't want to play it the same. We want to expand a little bit and try something different.

I've been going through a spiritual awakening my whole life, and several years back, I really got slapped in the head through different trials and tribulations in my marriage, and with my family. I finally came to a place where I had to come clean about a lot of things I was doing in my life, and I had to make some decisions. I realized at that point, there was something bigger going on in my life, and I need[ed] to go address it. I took a long, hard, deep dive into my faith and solidified whether I believed in it or not. Billy Joe has always had a strong faith. You can look at a lot of his writing and see that that's all of it. I admire the way that he lives his life. He's unique. I struggle with a lot of things every day, and I see that he may struggle with it too, but he knows where to go to get it right. It's beautiful. He hits on the truth. He's very grounded in being a mess of a man. He shines in being a screwed-up human, shines in his knowing, and knowing that he's loved. Sometimes he can't help himself doing the things he does, but there's no question to him who God is, and where God is in his life. He walks the walk I envy. It's inspiring.

When you see him play live, he speaks like a preacher, and the way that he can move a crowd makes him the whole package. You have guys that are great songwriters, singers, or performers. He's all of that—and [a] big personality. He's larger than life. He's the loudest guy in the room, [yet] he's the softest heart, the gentlest and kindest. But he won't take any lip from anybody. You don't guide him on where to go, he's going to clean up the mess behind him and make sure everybody's happy in the wake. There was a time onstage at Gruene Hall where he got off the mic and started preaching. It was almost like he was rapping, but poetically, with beautiful words. People were feeling the spirit coming through him. He knows the truth, and he knows the word. We're all cut from the same cloth, so deep down inside you either feel an attractiveness to the way someone's speaking or feel turned off by the way someone's speaking, and usually the attractiveness is that you finally found what you've been looking for. If you're turned off, it's because your heart is being dragged in the wrong direction. So when someone is speaking the truth to you, initially you don't want to hear that because deep down you realize you're going to have to make a pretty big change in your life to go in the direction that you need to go. That's where the negative draw comes from. We're talking foundational changes that [have] to be made, and, [when] people are afraid of that, they don't want to do it and look in the mirror and say, "The things you're doing in your life are wrong. The decisions you're making in your life are wrong." My change and awakening was awesome, and "Live Forever" has a deep meaning for me. Every time we play it, people know it. They sing along, feel it, and love it. A lot of them don't even know why they love it. It's because it's what he's saying is true.

Songwriting comes easy for Billy Joe. He came up to me at a show, and we knew we were going to see each other again in a week, and he wanted to get together between those times. He told me about [this] line he'd come up with, and I thought, *Man, that's a great line.* He goes, "Yeah, it's a good line. You want to write the song with me?" "Heck, yeah, I do!" It was one of the biggest, most honoring things that anybody's ever said to me. To have Billy Joe Shaver ask me to write a song with him, you can't be more flattered than that. We never did connect, and the next time I saw him I said, "I'm sorry we didn't connect. I'd really like to get with you to write it." He said, "Oh, heck, man. I already finished that one."

Dang! He doesn't stop and sit around and wonder what you're thinking or worry about. He's, "Oh. You didn't call? I'm feeling it. I know what to say. I know where the lyrics need to go, and here they are." They come right out of him. I doubt his writing pad has any scratch marks on it. I've seen it pour right out of him. The lyrics are perfectly portioned. We all have blessings. That's his, and his faith and love for life [need] to continue for future generations because he spreads a message that needs to be heard. It makes you want to stand up, clap your hands, and shout. When you put all that down and listen to it, you're inspired. Somebody else did something amazing. That tells you it's possible for you to do the same. You look at it and think, *Man, what am I capable of doing? Maybe I can do something amazing.* He spurs everyone around him to be better and excel. People are drawn to it. His music isn't going anywhere.[2]

Cory Morrow, born May 1, 1972, in Houston moved to Austin in 1993 to pursue a music career and released his debut Texas Time Travelin' *EP in 1997. He has since released ten studio albums, including his collaboration with Pat Green,* Songs We Wish We'd Written, *which was his first to chart. In 2005, Morrow contributed to the album* A Tribute to Billy Joe Shaver (Live) *with his version of "Live Forever," and his 2010 album,* Brand New Me, *hearkens back to Shaver as Morrow chronicles his newfound sobriety and celebrates his Christian faith.*

Jim Dalton (The Railbenders)

The Hickman-Dalton Gang was fortunate enough to open for Billy Joe Shaver in 2010 at a show in Denver. I was not sure I wanted to meet him because sometimes when you meet your heroes, you become disillusioned by the way they are in person. He's got a firm handshake, and he looked me in the eye with a smile like he knew me. There are some people who have charisma for miles. He's one of them. He let us share the only greenroom in the venue with him. He could not have been nicer. Billy Joe's had a huge impact on me. His songs speak to me. His influence on the way I write is greater than the most obvious songwriters. Bob Dylan is incredible, but I don't always feel a personal connection with his lyrics. He's from another planet. Billy Joe makes me feel like we live on the same street.

Jim Dalton.
Photo by
Mark Tepsic.

When I heard "Live Forever," I was all in. I had to go find every song I could get my hands on. It got me. The lyrics are just so damn good, and his ability to paint a picture with those words and melody makes it an effortless listen. I love his use of syllables, and I [pay attention to that] a lot. I once heard John Prine talk about the importance of syllables, and Dylan once said that songwriting is like doing a math problem. It's a numbering system, using the same number of syllables in verse lines, an effective tool for making it more memorable to the listener as well as the songwriter. Billy Joe's great at that. There are songs and stories that you want to hear told over and over again. "On a rainy Wednesday morning, that's the day that I was born in that old sharecropper's one-room country shack" paints a hell of a picture right from the bat. His songs have [stood the test of time] and always will stand the test of time.[3]

Jim Dalton is a singer, songwriter, and musician from Denver, Colorado. Dalton plays lead guitar for Roger Clyne and the Peacemakers, formerly the Refreshments, known for their nineties radio hits "Banditos" and "Down Together," as well as the theme song to the animated series King of the Hill. *He also fronts the Denver-based country band the Railbenders and cofounded the Hickman-Dalton Gang with Johnny Hickman of Cracker. In 2007, he played rhythm guitar for Bo Diddley. His solo shows are known for their loose, fun, sometimes serious, and often bawdy nature. He was inducted into the Arizona Music and Entertainment Hall of Fame as a member of Roger Clyne and the Peacemakers in 2019.*

Ann Duggan

We were visiting Austin, Texas, from England in 2011 and discovered him by reading an article about him in the *Austin Chronicle*. He was talking about his son [Eddy], who was an incredible guitar player. My guitarist Rob Hines took it upon himself to find out as much about him as possible, buying all the albums. Rob's guitar playing is in that same style, so [both Eddy] and Billy Joe were influences. The storytelling and the fact that it comes from the heart had quite an impact on us.

Whenever Billy Joe is over here, we try to catch him. I've seen him play three times here. First in London at the Borderline and then the Maze in Nottingham. Then we saw him outside of London. I wouldn't say that he's well-known here. The venues that he played were fairly small compared to if Willie Nelson came over. He's a bit of a niche market, really. I love the old country style of music. There's lots of people who do in this country. If they are into that, they know Waylon Jennings and Willie Nelson, the old guard. People love them over here, but it's strange in a way that Billy Joe Shaver doesn't seem to be in the that category. He is, but he isn't as recognized over here as much as they are. I don't know why. People may know the songs, but they don't know he's written them.

As a performer, Billy Joe is gritty. The songs carry everything. He's had a checkered past and lived quite a life. That living comes through and is within his songs. You don't get an awful lot of it these days. Storytelling doesn't figure in as much in popular music. Not in the way he and others like him do it. I'm not sure how much of that is going to apply in

Left to right: Rob Hines and Ann Duggan, promotional photo.

the future. It's something to be treasured. If his songs are preserved for another hundred years, I would hope that people look back and say, "My god, that's how to write a song. That guy must have felt that. I get it. I understand [his songs] because I [understand] where he's coming from and what he's saying." In one hundred years, if people understand that, they will learn and not keep dishing out songs that don't mean anything to anyone.

[Like Billy Joe] we try to tell stories within our songs and deliver them from a sense of ownership. We're not just singing about something. It's something that means something to you, that you've experienced. Songs about feelings have an effect on people. If people hear songs from the 1960s and 1970s, it brings back memories and means something, but there's songs that you don't remember from one year to the next. Townes Van Zandt's and Billy Joe's songs will last forever. If a song is done right, it lives forever, but if it's written with money in mind and to please the promoters, then where's the depth? Some of the best songwriters around have not made any money. Songwriting and performing is something you have to do, [because] there's nothing else you want to do. It's part of your makeup and life. That's what writers like them have that others don't.

We cover "Live Forever." We loved the sentiment. If you sing the song properly that should come over to the audience. We sing it as a ballad, a beautiful ballad and a song of hope. No matter what life throws at you, you can carry on. It's also about loss, and that goes very deep. That's why its affects people, and they feel what he must have felt when he wrote it. In my shows, I don't do "Live Forever" all the time, but when I do it, people get quite emotional. They have cried. It's a powerful song. When we saw him at the Borderline, I'd just recorded it, and we gave Billy Joe a CD of it. The next thing I know, it's on his website [that we had covered it]. We were very pleased that we were with so many distinguished performers. The fact that we're English, and it's a lot of Americans, we're privileged to spread the word if we can. We talk about him a lot and carry on his songs.[4]

Ann Duggan, born in Birmingham, England, is a singer-songwriter and front woman of the Ann Duggan Band. Over the years, she has slowly built a sizeable following in the United Kingdom and beyond, mixing influences from folk, blues, country, rock, and jazz. Duggan is known for her captivating style onstage and distinctive voice. She performs as a duo with guitarist Rob Hines, whose unique style has been compared to Richard Thompson and Rory Gallagher, among others. Her album If I Knew Then *includes a cover of Shaver's "Live Forever."*

Rod Picott

Billy Joe Shaver brought the party to Texas music with outlandish swagger, misbehaving, and a body of work any songwriter worth his soul would be amazed by. He rides a strange tightrope of humor and tragedy. It's braggadocio and self-deprecation, charming dark comedy that's humble and heartbreaking, very rarified air. It's the magic combination. I've tried my entire life to crack the code, and I haven't done it yet. I'm not sure if I'll ever get there.

Billy Joe has been a teacher to me, and I don't even know him. *Tramp on Your Street* changed my sense of what was possible with songwriting, and I loved Eddy's funk-ated, rollicking guitar playing. Billy Joe flourished with that band, and the title track is magic. He talks about going to see Hank Williams play as a kid: "He sang every song looking right

Rod Picott, Catfish Concerts, Austin, Texas, March 16, 2013. Photo by Brian T. Atkinson.

straight at me." What a moment to capture. It comes down to believability and authenticity. He uses the simple colloquial language of his days growing up in Texas. "Got a good Christian raising and an eight-grade education, ain't no need in y'all a-treatin' me this way," is beautiful and rolls off the tongue. I can't think of anyone else writing a line like that. Maybe John Prine, but Billy Joe is special. He gets his words across and could cover it all. He's powerful from one end to the other.

There are a lot of rock stars who make themselves seem larger than life. You can be Mick Jagger or Keith Richards, but you have the feeling that that's not really them. Pop music can be incredibly entertaining, but you have to be aware that there's a performer playing a character. You don't have that with Billy Joe. He's simultaneously himself and larger than life. Some artists are narcissistic and don't like to be countered. You can tell that they're worried about how you're perceiving them. When

Billy Joe's onstage, you get the feeling he's the same person as when he walks offstage. He is. He's like Abraham Lincoln, supremely confident and calm. You feel it in his presence. He's himself, and there's no one like him. Seeing him play "Live Forever" is special. I covered it in my own set, and I couldn't get through it. It's so moving and beautiful that I couldn't even cover it. I just couldn't get through it.[5]

Rod Picott, born November 3, 1964, in New Hampshire, was raised in New Berwick, Maine. In 1994, the alt-country and folk singer-songwriter relocated to Nashville, where he began playing local clubs, backing up artists such as Alisson Krauss. Picott released his debut album, Tiger Tom Dixon's Blues *in 2001 and through 2020 had released a total of twelve albums, including* Sew Your Heart with Wires *(2008) with frequent collaborator and touring partner Amanda Shires. The pair wrote "I Might Be Broken Now," on Picott's 2014 album,* Hang Your Hopes on a Crooked Nail, *about their breakup. Picott has published two books of poetry,* God in His Slippers *and* Murmuration.

Randy Rogers

Old Five and Dimers Like Me and *Freedom's Child* were the beginning of my musical journey in my formative years, and I started getting into songwriters. I was writing my own songs and playing them Wednesday nights down at Kent Finlay's Cheatham Street Warehouse in San Marcos. "Live Forever" spoke to me, and my band covered it. It's honest. Billy Joe is one of the greatest songwriters of his generation, an outlaw, and a gentleman. He describes things through his eyeballs. He's a no-bullshit, badass, blue-collar poet. His songs are introspective, true to the hardships and heartaches he endured since childhood, and stone-cold country.

I vividly remember playing a show with Billy Joe at Poor David's Pub in Dallas when he was on his acoustic tour. He drove himself and his dog to the gig in a four-door sedan. His dog was in the back going crazy. We were all scared to death to approach it, and Billy Joe just popped open his trunk and pulled out his guitar. He had about ten denim shirts in there. He takes his off, puts on an identical one, goes and plays the show. Billy Joe is a charismatic performer. His shows are like going to church.

Left to right: Kent Finlay and Randy Rogers, Cheatham Street Warehouse, San Marcos, Texas, June 9, 2014. Photo by Brian T. Atkinson.

My dad was a Baptist minister, so I connect when he goes up there, fire and brimstone. He's giving 110 percent, preaching the gospel of country music. He embodies the art form and is an influence getting other people to love his songs, cut them, and make them their own. It's what I aspire to do: three chords and the truth.

Randy Rogers, born August 23, 1979, in Celburne, Texas, is the front man for the Randy Rogers Band. Their 2000 debut album Live at Cheatham Street Warehouse *was recorded at that famed club in San Marcos. Through 2020 they had subsequently released ten studio albums, five of which charted in the Country Albums top ten. Their 2004 album* Rollercoaster *was produced by fellow Texas singer-songwriter Radney Foster, who also cowrote several songs, including "Tonight's Not the Night (for Goodbye)" which reached number forty-three. In 2006, they released their first major-label album,* Just a Matter of Time, *on Mercury Nashville. Randy Rogers Band had their first top-forty hit with "One More Sad Song" from* Trouble *(2013).*

Carson McHone

Billy Joe Shaver writes beautifully casual lines of profound emptiness that are key to great country songs because they aren't treated too preciously. "It Ain't Nothing New Babe" and "Ride Me Down Easy" are two songs that are country as hell. They're just great-feeling tunes, and the latter is really pretty rowdy and fun, but man do they pack a sad punch. "Live Forever" is one of the most beautiful songs ever written. It's incredible anyone could write and sing something so powerfully hopeful about such personal tragedy and heartbreak. It's a beautiful feat. The man's an outlaw, but it goes hand in hand. It's a gift to all of us.

I met Billy Joe at South by Southwest. He performed at the White Horse Tavern [in Austin], and I got to be right there at the front of the stage. He was in his Canadian tuxedo with that proud stance, and we were all packed in. He's a legend, and he commanded the stage as one. We just stared in awe the entire show. I felt very lucky to see him perform up close and personal. I stayed late to help clean up the chairs, and I came around the corner from out back with a stack of them, and almost plowed him over. I apologized profusely and told him I'd seen his show and loved his songs and signing. He said, "Oh, darlin'. I was singing for you." What a guy.[6]

Carson McHone. Photo by Tim Regan.

Carson McHone, born March 13, 1992, in Austin, Texas, released her debut EP Carson McHone *in 2013, and the following year she played South by Southwest for the first time. Shortly after, she received an invitation to join the inaugural class of the music documentary series* Project ATX6. *In 2015, McHone released her debut LP* Goodluck Man, *earning her a cover story in the* Austin Chronicle *as well as the support of Ray Wylie Hubbard, and she has shared the stage with such artists as Shaky Graves, Gary Clark Jr., and Joe Pug. Her second album,* Carousel *(2018), is dark and evocative honky-tonk inspired by such diverse sources as Bob Dylan, the Velvet Underground, and novelist Thomas Wolfe.*

Dallas Moore

Billy Joe Shaver's songwriting is timeless. He has a way of turning a phrase into poetry everyone can relate to. He rolls the sinning and saving all in the same song and delivers it up for you. It'll get you right. When I listen to his songs, I think, *Man, it's like he got in my head. I just lived what he wrote.* It might be a song from forty years ago, but it applies to me. He touches a lot of people that way. It's a gift. He's a master. My first introduction to his music was *Honky Tonk Heroes*, but I really got into him as he and Eddy started hitting it with *Tramp on Your Street*. It was electrified honky-tonk and gave them their unique sound. Eddy's guitar and Billy's voice were a match made in in heaven. Eddy was one of my guitar heroes, and when he died, it was the first time that something ever really hit me.

It wasn't long after he passed away that I first met Billy Joe. We were playing a show in Newport, Kentucky, at a place called the Southgate House [Revival], a honky-tonk in an old abandoned church. There's stained glass windows, and the altar is the stage. Billy Joe's performance was like a revival. His storytelling felt like redemption. After the show, I bought an album at his merch table, *Honky Tonk Heroes*, which was Billy, Waylon, Kristofferson, and Willie Nelson all doing Shaver songs. I gave him one of my albums and asked him to sign his for me. He said, "Well, you've got to sign yours for me." I did, and he offered me a cookie.

Billy Joe and I play a lot at a bar called Flora-Bama, which straddles the line of Florida and Alabama. The venue supports live music on five different stages, 365 days a year. If Billy's in the area and doesn't have a

Dallas Moore standing inside an abandoned church in Buffalo, New York. Photo by Mark Whitfield Lennon.

show booked, unannounced, he'll just walk in the bar and start playing. One of the last times he did that was before my great friend Wayne Mills was murdered. Wayne was playing up there, and here comes Billy Joe. Wayne's band knew all the songs, so Billy did a whole hour-long set.

The longest I'd ever seen him play was when we did the Last Honky Tonk Music Series at Pivo's Ice House down in Fayetteville, Texas. I'll never forget it. It was like getting saved. It's where I came up with the line, "I was baptized by bourbon and Billy Joe Shaver." The show was going to be the last date of Billy's tour. Less than a half mile from where the festival was going on, a tornado hit that morning, and it did some pretty bad damage to the local farmhouses, so we didn't know if the show was going to go on or not. The weather was suspect, but here comes Billy Joe onto the grounds. The sun comes out, and the clouds parted. He was having health issues at the time but got up and played [almost three hours] nonstop. He was full-tilt boogie, drawing you in with stories that'll hit you right between the mother and the fucker. When his agent found out, he called the people who booked the show and said, "Why did you make him play so long?" "We couldn't get him to stop."

On any given night, we do a ton of Billy songs. "Black Rose," "Hottest Thing in Town," "Omaha," "Honky Tonk Heroes"—I can go on and on. Sometimes I'll go on a tear of 'em. My mom and dad were married sixty-two and a half years, and they recently passed away six and a half weeks apart. Mama played music, and we'd always sing "Live Forever" together. She loved that song. Since then, we've ended our shows with it. I've had "Live Forever" tattooed on my arm for twenty years. Billy's songwriting and musical influence is profound, but he's also an influence on a personal level. He's a father figure to a lot of us. That isn't him trying to be a mentor, it's who he is. He'll give you advice, help you kick the can a little [farther] down the road, and encourage you to be yourself. There's zero bullshit with him. Billy did everything his way. He stayed true to himself, good, bad or ugly, and wrote the canon of country music. A hundred years after Billy leaves this earthly world, people are still going to be singing his songs. He's never gonna die.[7]

Dallas Moore, is a Cincinnati-based outlaw country singer-songwriter who grew up on the music of Hank Williams and Elvis Presley. Moore released his debut album My Heroes Have Always Been Cowboys *in 1991. Known for his gruff vocals and southern-fried honky-tonk, Moore is a two-time Ameripolitan Award winner in the categories of Outlaw Country Male and Honky Tonk Male. Moore cites Billy Joe Shaver as a primary influence, and the song "Outlaw Country" from his 2009 album* Can't Tame a Wildcat *pays tribute to Billy Joe Shaver, name-checking him along with the album* Honky Tonk Heroes. *His 2019 album* Tryin' to Be a Blessing *features the first studio recording of his classic "Mama and Daddy," a commentary on his mother's hardcore Christian faith and his father's hard-living ways.*

Jim Lauderdale

I first saw Billy Joe Shaver back in 1980 when I was living up in New York City. He's strong, larger than life, a big presence, and has this special "it" factor few have. He's complex in his simplicity. He can say so much with just the right words. I admire that. He's a naturally gifted poet, and he can really rock without changing who he is. He's just doing his thing, and it fits in with the rest of his music. In some ways, Billy Joe is this unknown person to the masses. Outlaws like Waylon and Willie drew a lot from the essence of him. They respected him. Waylon made those songs his own. It was a perfect match of material and artist. Just perfect.

Jim Lauderdale, Music City Roots Stage, AmericanaFest, Nashville, Tennessee, September 14, 2017. Photo by Mark Whitfield Lennon.

Billy Joe set the course for a lot of songwriters and performers. I'm always in awe of him, and he's always been very welcoming and put me at ease.

When the great Donald Lindley—who played drums with me, Lucinda Williams, Duane Jarvis, and Rosie Flores—passed away, there was a memorial at the Sutler Saloon in Nashville, and a bunch of us played. Billy Joe came and did "Live Forever" a capella. It uplifted everybody and gave comfort to a lot of us, including Donald's wife Kathy, who really appreciated it. I'll never forget that. We were torn up about losing Donald, and Billy Joe lightened our hearts.

The last time I saw Billy Joe perform was a few months back [in 2018] at the Grand Ole Opry. It was a full house. Billy Joe had this twinkle in his eye and full control onstage. He had command of the audience. He's very strong, and I was marveling at how loose his body was and how centered he was. He looked fresh as anytime I've seen him. I was taken by it. He's always been extremely kind to me and made me feel accepted because he's got a pretty high level of greatness and people can easily be intimidated by that. Through the years, we started working together and playing shows, but I did not lose my awe of him. I still have it. He's left his mark.[8]

Jim Lauderdale, born April 11, 1957, in Troutman, North Carolina, is a Grammy-winning, Nashville-based songwriter whose songs have been recorded by artists including George Strait, Elvis Costello, the Dixie Chicks, Vince Gill, and Patty Loveless. Since starting his career as a recording artist in 1986, he has released thirty-one studio albums. He cohosts The Buddy & Jim Show *on SiriusXM Outlaw Country with longtime friend Buddy Miller, with whom he collaborated on the 2013 New West Records album* Buddy & Jim, *which charted in the top one hundred country albums.*

Elizabeth Cook

I was on Music Row at my publishing company in the midst of the nineties money grab, and Billy Joe had come down there. The executives were sitting in their corner suites making million-dollar-a-year salaries. Meanwhile, the legend who started the outlaw movement and was Waylon Jennings's musical muse was out on Sixteenth Avenue with the hood of his broke-down truck up and trying to fix it. You play nice and kiss ass to the gate holders in Nashville, [but] Billy Joe's a rebel.

Left to right: Tyler Cooney and Elizabeth Cook after a show at the Sportsmen's Tavern, Buffalo, New York, October 27, 2019. Photo courtesy of Tyler Cooney.

He's authentic. He doesn't think about being a brand or being on brand. He's a threat to the pussies that run things, a badass who will shoot a fucker if somebody ain't acting right.

I didn't grow up in most literate of cultures coming from the Deep South, so Billy Joe was someone to aspire to be. My mother, who was a singer-songwriter, used to [perform] "Old Five and Dimers (Like Me)." He must have been struck by lightning. He writes poetry in a way that only he can. It speaks for the deeply rural people and resonates. I opened for him at festival in Poland. The crowd was rowdy and rural as hell. They were next-level rednecks, the closest likeness to Billy Joe that I've seen. Billy Joe really connected with them. It was a wild, scary scene.

I was recently at the *Outlaws and Armadillos* opening at the Country Music Hall of Fame. I was in my dressing room with Tanya Tucker and her daughter Presley, and when Billy Joe came on, we gathered around the monitor, cranked it, and sang along. We were just enjoying him, trying to soak him in, and celebrating him. Billy is vastly underrated, and acceptance hasn't been the mantra of his career, but that night in Nashville at the Hall of Fame, everyone was celebrating him. He could sense that appreciation. He was very happy. It was wonderful to see.[9]

Elizabeth Cook, born July 17, 1972, in Wildwood, Florida, is a Nashville-based singer-songwriter and acclaimed live performer. She hosts the show Apron Springs *on SiriusXM Outlaw Country Radio and is a frequent guest star on long-running hit cartoon series* Squidbillies *on the Cartoon Network's Adult Swim. Cook made her Grand Ole Opry debut on March 17, 2000, and has since made over four hundred appearances there.*

David Lee

Billy Joe Shaver is my hero in life. I met him when I first got to Nashville. I had four hundred dollars and a brand-new wife, and we moved into these junky little old apartments called Iroquois Apartments in [nearby] Bellevue. Going to Nashville to be a songwriter, I was thinking, *You're going to starve in the beginning, but you're going to have hits and stay positive. You're going to make your way through this.* That day, I went to take the trash out, and I saw Eddy Shaver standing there, throwing his trash in the trashcan before me. I said, "Are you Eddy?" He looked at

Left to right:
Billy Joe Shaver
and David Lee,
Riley's Tavern,
Hunter, Texas,
December 8,
2017. Photo by
Stacie Lee.

me and said, "Yeah." I said, "Hey man. My name is David." I heard Billy go, "Eddy!" He's hollering at him, and I look up, and right across the breezeway in a different apartment was Billy standing over the rail, and I said, "Do y'all live here?" "Yes." In that moment, I saw his beat-up old van. There's my hero right next to me. For a kid, it was, *Oh my gosh*. I was being made aware of what the music business really was. It stripped away all the facade immediately.

The second time I met Billy Joe was in the bathroom at the [2003] BMI Awards. I was there getting an award for a song I'd written that Mark Wills put out called "19 Somethin'." I was standing at the urinal, and Billy walks up right beside me. I glanced over and thought, *Holy cow*. My heart's beating, and I want to say something, but what do you say at a urinal? Most of the time guys don't stand and talk there, but I had to say something. I'm looking at the wall and say, "Billy? What was that song 'Black Rose' about?" "It's about sleeping with an old black gal back in Texas." It made total sense. We were at the NSAI [Nashville Songwriters Association International] Awards another time with our heroes like Guy Clark. Billy Joe gave a speech. He walks up to the mic and says, "If you don't love Jesus, go to Hell." Then he walked off. It was a moment of "This guy does not give a damn." We went outside to see and talk to him [after]. My friend's wife was pregnant. He put his hand on her belly with the cut-off fingers.

Seeing Billy Joe through the years, he always recognizes me. He played last year over at Riley's in New Braunfels. I went to see him. He'd fallen two weeks before and cut his face. He had one hundred stitches, and he went onstage with blood on his shirt. There were only about forty people that showed up. It was shocking. He played two nights in a row, because they figured he'd sell out back-to-back. I went both nights. The first night, he walked over, looked at me, stopped, and stared, out of place. He said, "Was I in a movie with you?" I said, "No. I have been following you all my life." He said, "Well, man, it's really good to see you." I told him I moved back to Texas like he had. The next night at the show, he got offstage and he said, "Man, you'd think more people would know me by now." I said, "Billy, everybody knows you. We spent years writing songs in Nashville, and I can't tell you how many times we would say, 'What would Billy Joe say right here? What would he do?' [We're] chasing those songs every day. You're a hero. I just want you to know that."

He stared off like he was taking it in. I don't think he realizes how big of an impact he was on us young songwriters, even the ones on Music Row that were writing commercial music. He was never a tool for the machine like we are today. He never tried to fit the system. He always inspired us with his writing. On "Ride Me Down Easy" [he sings], "Leave word in the dust where I lay," imagery that I took into my own writing. The way he speaks is so unique. His words are from another time, and with his use of word dichotomy, nouns, and verbs, he doesn't say it, he shows it. It's poetry. He's an out-of-the-dust cowboy, distinctly his own.

I have a big picture of me and him on the wall of my writing room. I use that to inspire me because when I don't know what to say, I know how to find it, because I've listened enough to what he did as a writer. I wrote a song called "I Need You" with Tony Lane. We're like brothers, and both of us were Billy Joe fanatics. A lot of the stuff we wrote was after him. Because it was like something Billy would write, we didn't think anybody would record it. Somehow Faith Hill and Tim McGraw did, and it got nominated for a Grammy. There's a line in there, "I need you like a needle needs a vein and my Uncle Joe in Oklahoma needs rain." It's the use of the use of pictures. Showing it, not saying it. That's the most unique gift Billy was given. It's not something that he learned, it's what we've learned from him as writers, and everyone in the business is better because of him, whether they know it or not. You say what you want to without worrying about what people think. One of the publishers tried to get us to change the "needle needs a vein" line. The other publisher said, "Heck, no. That's going to make everybody take notice." You see that in Billy's writing. He has unique lines that stand out and make a whole song colorful with words like "I'm just an old chunk of coal, but I'm gonna be a diamond someday."

In the modern world, you have to be careful with what you say. You have to pare down and say it on a third-grade level for people to understand it. I've fought that tooth and nail for my twenty-four years in Nashville. I fought that every day because of coming out of the style of writers like Guy Clark, and Townes, and Billy, and these guys in Texas that I grew up listening to. I love all those guys, but I relate to Billy Joe the most. He's singing about stuff I know about. I grew up doing construction work, and Billy Joe sings [on "Manual Labor" from *Salt of the Earth*], "The government thinks manual labor ain't nothing but a Mexican." He's taking things out of our lives and making them funny and thought-provoking.

Billy Joe takes me [somewhere] in his music. "Willy the Wandering Gypsy and Me" is a perfect example of a song where you hear it, and you feel like you're out on the road. You want to be with those two guys, rolling down the road. "[Willy], you're wild as a Texas blue norther, ready rolled from the same makings as me." It's the alliteration and pictures. Guy told great stories and had great moments in his songs, but Billy didn't waste a word. He nails it. It's as good as you can possibly make it. He's the most honest human in a world of plastic musicians. I see him every chance I can, because he's what we all want to be. He is something. He's not punching at the wind. He's either trying to save your soul with Jesus, or he's trying to kick your ass. Billy Joe is a contradiction.

I saw him at [the] Roundup in Boerne, Texas. Alex Harvey is a great songwriter who's known him over the years, and he was there. Billy's onstage, and he says, "I think I'm going to die up here tonight." He was standing there, wobbling, and then he walked off the back of the stage funny. I ran around, and we're running up the ramp, and he says, "Call an ambulance." Then the owner was running inside, and Billy said, "Wait, just get me to the car and get me some water." We got him water, got him in the car. He cooled down, and he started feeling better, but we thought, *With his life, and story, he's going to die onstage*. It would be a fitting end to a crazy journey.

Billy Joe doesn't get the recognition he should, and it breaks my heart. I go to shows and think, *What is wrong with you people?* You go out to a Koe Wetzel show, and there are ten thousand people. Billy Joe [draws] forty people? We lost our culture. The culture of writing is getting lost. It's sad. We're in jeopardy of losing an entire industry. We don't need to forget Billy or Townes or Guy. We don't need to forget the names of the guys that blazed the trail. Show up at a Billy Joe Shaver concert. Buy his records, and support what he's been doing for forty years. He's going to be remembered alongside the greats like Bob Dylan and Tom T. Hall. People need to study him to learn how to be honest. I always go back to that with him, because he's as real as it gets. It's what connects with people. A lot of the writing we have today is superficial, just words on paper, a collection of lines. If you're serious about wanting to understand the craft and what it means to be a writer, you're going to have to stop at Billy Joe Shaver. He [should] go down as the greatest country songwriter to ever put pen to paper.[10]

David Lee, born in Wichita Falls, Texas, is a Grammy-nominated, multi-award-winning songwriter who cut his teeth in Texas honky-tonks, playing a mix of blues and country. Lee moved to Nashville in 1993, when he signed his first publishing deal. His first top-ten hits came with Lee Ann Womack's "(Now You See Me) Now You Don't" in 1999, followed by Brad Martin's "Before I Knew Better" in 2002. In 2003, David signed with BMG Music Publishing and cowrote his number-one hit song, "19 Somethin'" for Mark Wills as well as "Letters From Home" for John Michael Montgomery. He received a Song of the Year Grammy nomination for Tim McGraw and Faith Hill's riveting love song "I Need You," followed by second number-one hit "Lucky Man," performed by Montgomery Gentry. In 2012, David signed with Ten-Ten Music Group (Barry Coburn), and in 2014 and 2015 he had two number-one songs on the Texas charts by artist Cody Johnson, "Me and My Kind" and "Cowboy Like Me." In 2015, Alabama cut two of Lee's songs, "Come Find Me" and their first radio single in over fourteen years, "I Wasn't through Lovin' You Yet."

Billy Joe Shaver, City Winery, Nashville, Tennessee. Photo by Kathy Reid-Papson.

Afterword

This book's interviews, conducted 2018–19, often echo notions of Billy Joe Shaver's immortality. He was folklore in his own time. I doubt that anyone believed he would live forever in physical form, but it almost seemed possible. He was transcendent in his presence and his words. Of course, Shaver understood and embraced his own mortality—"Gonna reach a new heaven, higher than high; When I get my wings, hey I'm gonna fly," he sang on "When I Get My Wings."

As he spread the gospel on recordings and atop barroom stages, he'd also sing a line like "The devil made me do it the first time, the second time I done it on my own." He owned up to his faults. He was honest and gave the world the gift of his songs.

Billy Joe Shaver wasn't your typical evangelist preacher, shooting a man in the face the same day photos were taken for the cover of his Grammy-nominated gospel album. His life was like literature, and his favorite book was the Bible. I can only imagine that Shaver found comfort in Romans 7:22–25 as Paul the Apostle describes the conflict of two natures.

> For I joyfully concur with the law of God in the inner man, but I see a different law in the members of my body, waging war against the law of my mind and making me a prisoner of the law of sin which is in my members. Wretched man that I am. Who will set me free from the body of this death? Thanks be to God through Jesus Christ our Lord. So then, on the one hand I myself with my mind am serving the law of God, but on the other, with my flesh the law of sin.

Billy Joe Shaver wasn't perfect, but the words in his songs always were. This book wasn't meant to end with an afterword. When I first completed the manuscript, Shaver was alive and David Lee's words were just right. My goal with this book was to help preserve Billy Joe Shaver's songwriting legacy, even if only in a small way. It was an honor to do so, but I realize that no one could summarize Shaver's songwriting legacy better or more simply than he did: "Just like the songs I leave behind me, I'm gonna live forever now."

—Courtney Lennon
May 17, 2021

Notes

Introduction

1. Brian Wright, interview with Courtney S. Lennon, March 12, 2019.

2. Billy Joe Shaver, *Honky Tonk Hero* (Austin: University of Texas Press, 2005), back cover.

3. Paul Kingsbury, Michael McCall, and John W. Rumble, *The Encyclopedia of Country Music*, 2nd ed. (New York: Oxford University Press, 2012), 456.

4. Billy Joe Shaver, "I Been to Georgia on a Fast Train," on *Old Five and Dimers Like Me,* 1973, Monument Record Corp.

5. Joe Holley, "Billy Joe Shaver: Sin and Salvation Poet," in *Pickers and Poets: The Ruthlessly Poetic Singer-Songwriters of Texas*, edited by Craig Clifford and Craig D. Hills (College Station: Texas A&M University Press, 2016), 86.

6. Don McCleese, "Gospel According to Billy Joe," *Texas Music*, Summer 2014, 41.

7. Kimmie Rhodes, interview with Courtney S. Lennon, August 3, 2019.

8. Billy Joe Shaver, "Tramp on Your Street," on *Tramp on Your Street* (Zoo/ Praxis, 1993).

9. Michael Franklin, "An Interview with Billy Joe Shaver," *Amplifier*, August 6, 2012, www.bgamplifier.com/.

10. Terry Paul Roland, "Shaver and His Maker: From Hell-Bound Honky Tonk Hero to Holy-Roller," *Turnstyled, Junkpiled*, July 30, 2012, http://turnstyledjunk piled.com/2012/07/30/shaver-and-his-maker-the-tj-interview.

11. Bill C. Malone and Tracey E. W. Laird, *Country Music USA*, 50th anniv. ed. (Austin: University of Texas Press, 2018), 465.

12. Roland, "Shaver and His Maker."

13. Roland, "Shaver and His Maker."

14. Malone and Laird, *Country Music USA*, 50th anniv. ed., 472.

15. Chuck Mead, interview with Courtney S. Lennon, June 21, 2019.

16. Geoff Edgers, "Billy Joe Shaver Invented Outlaw Country Music. Why Is He Still Rambling around Texas in a Van?" *Washington Post*, March 15, 2018.

17. Billy Joe Shaver, "Willy the Wandering Gypsy and Me," on *Old Five and Dimers Like Me* (Monument Record, 1973).

18. James Scott Bullard, interview with Courtney S. Lennon, July 18, 2018. See also www.jamesscottbullard.com.

19. Brian T. Atkinson, "The Gospel of Billy Joe Shaver's Timeless Lyrics Preach Secular Sermon of Faith in Life and in the People You Love," *Austin 360*, September 24, 2012, www.austin360.com/.

20. David Lee, interview with Courtney S. Lennon, September 17, 2018.

21. Quoted in "Billy Joe Shaver—88.1 KDHX Welcomes," www.oldrockhouse.com/event/billy-joe-shaver, July 18, 2014.

22. Michael Hall, "Billy Joe Shaver, the Blustery Tenderhearted Country Star Known as the 'Wacko from Waco,' Dies of a Stroke," *Texas Monthly*, December 2020, www.texasmonthly.com/arts-entertainment/billy-joe-shaver-death.

23. Joseph Hudak, "Billy Joe Shaver on His Outlaw Life and Hard-Fought Comeback," *Rolling Stone*, December 5, 2014.

Hard to Be an Outlaw

1. Rodney Crowell, interview with Courtney S. Lennon, July 6, 2018. See also www.rodneycrowell.com.

2. Bobby Bare Jr., interview with Courtney S. Lennon, July 31, 2018. See also www.bobbybarejr.com.

3. Harold Eggers Jr. with L. E. McCullough, *My Years with Townes Van Zandt: Music, Genius and Rage* (Milwaukee: Back Beat Books, 2018), 40–41.

4. Harold Eggers Jr., interview with Courtney S. Lennon, September 30, 2018. For more on Townes Van Zandt and Billy Joe Shaver, see Brian T. Atkinson, *I'll Be Here in the Morning: The Songwriting Legacy of Townes Van Zandt* (College Station: Texas A&M University Press), 43–49.

5. Billy Don Burns, interview with Courtney S. Lennon, September 17, 2019. See also www.billydonburns.net.

6. Ray Wylie Hubbard, interview with Courtney S. Lennon, May 8, 2018. See also Brian T. Atkinson, *The Messenger: The Songwriting Legacy of Ray Wylie Hubbard* (College Station: Texas A&M University Press, 2019); and www.raywyliehubbard.com.

7. Lee Roy Parnell, interview with Courtney S. Lennon, August 23, 2019. See also www.leeroyparnell.com.

8. Steve Earle, liner notes for Billy Joe Shaver, *Long in the Tooth* (Lightning Rod Records, 2014).

9. Steve Earle, interview with Courtney S. Lennon, September 20, 2018. See also www.steveearle.com.

Honky Tonk Heroes

1. Jessi Colter, interview with Courtney S. Lennon, May 17, 2019. See also www.officialjessicolter.com.

2. Ray Benson, interview with Courtney S. Lennon, July 10, 2019. See also www.asleepatthewheel.com.

3. Kinky Friedman, interview with Courtney S. Lennon, July 6, 2018. See also www.kinkyfriedman.com.

4. Whey Jennings, interview with Courtney S. Lennon, June 14, 2019. See also www.facebook.com/w.a.jennings.

5. Ted Russell Kamp, interview with Courtney S. Lennon, June 20, 2018. See also www.tedrussellkamp.com.

6. Mark Chesnutt, interview with Courtney S. Lennon, October 7, 2019. See markchesnutt.com.

7. James Carothers, interview with Courtney S. Lennon, June 26, 2018. See also "James Carothers," Grand Ole Opry, www.opry.com/artists/james-carothers.

I Been to Georgia on a Fast Train

1. J. P. Harris, interview with Courtney S. Lennon, September 24, 2019. See also Harris's website, ilovehonkytonk.com.

2. Matt Minglewood, interview with Courtney S. Lennon, September 9, 2020. See also www.mattminglewood.com.

3. Vincent Neil Emerson, interview with Courtney S. Lennon, September 13, 2018. See also www.vincentneilemerson.com.

4. Robert Ellis, interview with Courtney S. Lennon, September 25, 2019. See also Ellis's website www.texaspianoman.com.

5. Mando Saenz, interview with Courtney S. Lennon, September 27, 2019. See also www.mandosaenzmusic.com.

6. Cecil Allen Moore, email interview with Courtney S. Lennon, September 22, 2019. See also www.cecilallenmoore.com.

Everybody's Brother

1. John Carter Cash, interview with Courtney S. Lennon, August 10, 2018. See also www.johncartercash.com.

2. Marty Stuart, interview with Courtney S. Lennon, November 30, 2018. See also www.martystuart.net.

3. Steve Earle, liner notes for Billy Joe Shaver, *Long in the Tooth* (Lightning Rod Records, 2014).

4. James McMurtry, interview with Courtney S. Lennon, June 13, 2019. See also www.jamesmcmurtry.com.

5. Kimmie Rhodes, interview with Courtney S. Lennon, August 3, 2019. See also www.kimmierhodes.com.

6. Richie Allbright, interview with Courtney S. Lennon, August 12, 2019. See also www.facebook.com/richieallbrightmusic.

7. Terri Hendrix, interview with Courtney S. Lennon, August 12, 2019. See also www.terrihendrix.com.

8. Chuck Mead, interview with Courtney S. Lennon, June 21, 2019. See also www.chuckmead.com.

Tramp on Your Street

1. Jesse Dayton, interview with Courtney S. Lennon, July 30, 2018. See also www.jessedayton.com.

2. Keith Christopher, interview with Courtney S. Lennon, October 3, 2019.

3. David Waddell, email interview with Courtney S. Lennon, September 2, 2019. See also "David Waddell and Hellbound Train," ReverbNation, www.reverbnation.com/davidwaddellhellboundtrain.

4. Rosie Flores, interview with Courtney S. Lennon, August 2, 2018. See also www.rosieflores.com.

5. Brian Molnar, interview with Courtney S. Lennon, September 15, 2019. See also www.brianmolnar.com.

6. Radney Foster, interview with Courtney S. Lennon, May 28, 2019. See also www.radneyfoster.com.

7. Bruce Robison, interview with Courtney S. Lennon, June 16, 2018. See also www.brucerobison.com.

8. Jeremy Lynn Woodall, interview with Courtney S. Lennon, August 14, 2019. See also www.facebook.com/JLWGrinders.

9. Adam Carter, interview with Courtney S. Lennon, August 13, 2019. See also www.facebook.com/AdamCarterGuitarist.

10. Brian Whelan, interview with Courtney S. Lennon, November 8, 2019. See also www.brianwhelanmusic.com.

11. Jason McKenzie, interview with Courtney S. Lennon, October 2, 2018. See also www.atash.com.

Wacko from Waco

1. "Billy Joe Shaver Posts Bond in Alleged Shooting, Versions of Incident Differ," *Country Standard Time*, April 4, 2007.

2. Michael Hoinski, "A Conversation with Billy Joe Shaver," *Texas Monthly*, April 30, 2011, https://www.texasmonthly.com/articles/a-conversation-with-billy-joe-shaver.

3. Tracie Ferguson, email interview with Courtney S. Lennon.

4. Patrick Doyle, "Billy Joe Shaver Found Not Guilty for Shooting: On the Scene in Waco," *Rolling Stone*, April 12, 2010.

5. Hoinski, "Conversation with Billy Joe Shaver."

6. Trigger Coroneos, "Billy Joe Shaver Found Not Guilty!!!," *Saving Country Music*, April 9, 2010, https://www.savingcountrymusic.com/billy-joe-shaver-found-not-guilty.

7. Sheldon Bernie, "Billy Joe Shaver: The Last Outlaw in Country Music," *Vice*, December 16, 2016, https://www.vice.com/en/article/69pk8r/billy-joe-shaver-the-last-outlaw-in-country-music.

8. Hoinski, "Conversation with Billy Joe Shaver."

9. "Billy Joe Shaver Posts Bond in Alleged Shooting."

10. Brian T. Atkinson, email interview with Courtney S. Lennon, November 23, 2019.

11. Tommy Witherspoon, "Country Crooner Billy Joe Shaver's Aggravated Assault Trial Slated to Begin Today," *Waco Tribune-Herald*, April 6, 2010.

12. Michael Hall, "The Trials of Billy Joe Shaver," *Texas Monthly*, March 30, 2010. https://www.texasmonthly.com/arts-entertainment/the-trials-of-billy-joe-shaver; Tommy Witherspoon, "UPDATE: Willie Nelson, Actor Robert Duvall at Billy Joe Shaver's Trial," *Waco Tribune-Herald*, April 8, 2010.

13. Coroneos, "Billy Joe Shaver Found Not Guilty!!!"

14. Patrick Doyle, "Q&A: Billy Joe Shaver on His Career, Suicide Attempt and Waco," *Rolling Stone*, July 23, 2012.

15. TheCwhatudid, "Billy Joe Shaver and Dale Watson," *YouTube*, Apr 11, 2010.

16. Dale Watson, interview with Courtney S. Lennon, May 4, 2018.

17. Coroneos, "Billy Joe Shaver Found Not Guilty!!!"

18. Dale Watson interview. See also www.dalewatson.com.

19. Nick Gaitan, interview with Courtney S. Lennon, September 25, 2019. See also www.facebook.com/NickGaitanMusic.

20. Brian Wright, interview with Courtney S. Lennon, March 12, 2019. See also www.brianwrightandthesneakups.com.

21. Wayne Hancock, interview with Courtney S. Lennon, July 14, 2018. See also www.waynehancock.com.

22. Tim Easton, interview with Courtney S. Lennon, January 27, 2020. See also www.timeaston.com.

Get Thee behind Me, Satan

1. Michael Ubaldini, email interview with Courtney S. Lennon, October 1, 2019. See also www.rocknrollpoet.com.

2. Aaron Watson, interview with Courtney S. Lennon, August 24, 2019. See also www.aaronwatson.com.

3. Jason Charles Miller, interview with Courtney S. Lennon, June 24, 2018. See also www.jasoncharlesmiller.com.

4. Brennen Leigh, interview with Courtney S. Lennon, September 23, 2019. See www.brennenleigh.net.

91. Bonnie Montgomery, interview with Courtney S. Lennon, September 20, 2019. See also www.bonniemontgomerymusic.com.

Salt of the Earth

1. Roger Alan Wade, interview with Courtney S. Lennon, June 27, 2018. See www.facebook.com/OfficialRogerAlanWade.

2. Jonathan Tyler, interview with Courtney S. Lennon, July 31, 2018. See also www.jonathantylermusic.com.

3. Jackson Taylor, interview with Courtney S. Lennon, June 27, 2018. See also www.officialjacksontaylor.com.

4. Stoney LaRue, interview with Courtney S. Lennon, September 26, 2019. See also www.stoneylarue.com.

5. Matt Harlan interview with Courtney S. Lennon, June 22, 2018. See also www.mattharlan.com.

6. Scott H. Biram, interview with Courtney S. Lennon, June 20, 2019. See also www.scotthbiram.com.

7. Gethen Jenkins, interview with Courtney S. Lennon, June 21, 2018. See also www.gethenjenkinsmusic.com.

8. Ben Reddell, email interview with Courtney S. Lennon, September 24, 2019. See also www.benreddellband.com.

9. Chris Fullerton, interview with Courtney S. Lennon, June 26, 2018. See also www.chrisfullerton.com.

Live Forever

1. John Rich, interview with Courtney S. Lennon, May 10, 2019. See also www.bigandrich.com.

2. Cory Morrow, interview with Courtney S. Lennon, June 19, 2018. See also www.corymorrow.com.

3. Jim Dalton, email interview with Courtney S. Lennon. See also www.jimdaltonmusic.com.

4. Ann Duggan, interview with Courtney S. Lennon, January 25, 2020. See also www.annduggan.co.uk.

5. Rod Picott, interview with Courtney S. Lennon, November 28, 2018. See also www.rodpicott.com.

6. Carson McHone, email interview with Courtney S. Lennon. See also www.carsonmchonemusic.com.

7. Dallas Moore, interview with Courtney S. Lennon, June 23, 2018. See also www.dallasmoore.com.

8. Jim Lauderdale, interview with Courtney S. Lennon, January 22, 2019. See also www.jimlauderdalemusic.com.

9. Elizabeth Cook, interview with Courtney S. Lennon, July 17, 2019. See also www.elizabeth-cook.com.

10. David Lee, interview with Courtney S. Lennon, September 17, 2018. See also www.davidleemusic.com.

Selected Discography

Studio Albums

Old Fiver and Dimers Like Me, Monument, 1973

When I Get My Wings, Capricorn, 1976

Gypsy Boy, Capricorn, 1977

*I'm Just an Old Chunk of Coal (but I'm Gonna Be a
Diamond Someday)*, Columbia, 1981

Billy Joe Shaver, Columbia, 1982

Salt of the Earth, Columbia, 1987

Tramp on Your Street, Volcano, 1993

Highway of Life, Justice, 1996

Victory, New West, 1998

Electric Shaver, New West, 1999

The Earth Rolls On, New West, 2001

Freedom's Child, Compadre, 2002

Try and Try Again, Compadre, 2003

Billy and the Kid, Compadre, 2004

The Real Deal, Compadre, 2005

Everybody's Brother, Compadre, 2007

Long in the Tooth, Lightning Rod Records, 2014

Live Albums

Unshaven: Live at Smith's Olde Bar, Volcano, 1995

Live from Down Under (with Kinky Friedman), Sphincter, 2003

A Tribute to Billy Joe Shaver: Live, Compadre, 2005

Storyteller: Live at the Blue Bird, Sugar Hill, 2007

Live at Billy Bob's Texas, Smith Music Group 2012

Live from Austin, TX: Austin City Limits, New West, 2012

Index